Richard Crashaw

Carmen Deo Nostro

Te decet hymnus, sacred poems

Richard Crashaw

Carmen Deo Nostro

Te decet hymnus, sacred poems

ISBN/EAN: 9783741103780

Manufactured in Europe, USA, Canada, Australia, Japa

Cover: Foto ©Andreas Hilbeck / pixelio.de

Manufactured and distributed by brebook publishing software (www.brebook.com)

Richard Crashaw

Carmen Deo Nostro

CARMEN DEO NOSTRO.

*Dressed in the glorious madness of a Muse,
Whose feet can walk the Milky-way, and choose
Her starry throne; whose holy heats can warm
The grave, and hold up an exalted arm
To lift me from my lazy urn, to climb
Upon the stooped shoulders of old Time,
And trace eternity.*

TO THE MORNING.

Carmen

Deo Nostro

TE DECET HYMNUS

Sacred Poems

By Richard Crashaw

EDITED, WITH AN INTRODUCTION, BY

J. R. TUTIN.

LONDON :
WILLIAM ANDREWS & CO., 5, FARRINGDON AVENUE.

Introduction.

I. BIOGRAPHICAL.

RICHARD CRASHAW was the son of the Reverend William Crashaw, D.D., by his first wife, and was born in London, 1612-13. The precise date of his birth it is impossible to ascertain, and the known facts of his life are few. He was admitted to the University of Cambridge at the age of eighteen, that is, about the year 1630, and elected a scholar of Pembroke Hall, so his biographer Willmott informs us, March 26, 1632. He took the degree B.A., in 1634, the same year publishing his first volume, a collection of Latin Epigrams, and other poems, which was inscribed to Benjamin Laney, the Master of Pembroke Hall. A studious, poetical, and religious life he led at the University, and spent several hours a day in the quietude of St. Mary's Church. "In the Temple of God, under His wing, he led his life, in St. Mary's Church, near St. Peter's College: there he lodged under Tertullian's roof of angels; there he made his nest more gladly than David's swallow near the house of God, where, like a primitive saint, he offered more prayers in the night than others usually offer in the day." (Preface to *Steps to the Temple*, 1646.)

In November, 1636, he passed to Peterhouse, of which he was made a Fellow in 1637, and Master of Arts in

1638, with a view of entering Holy Orders. He soon became a powerful preacher, his high and rich qualities, and his enthusiasm, abundantly evident in all his writings, rendering him an effective and popular religious teacher.

But troublous days were fast approaching. The year 1644 saw the University of Cambridge converted into a garrison for the Parliament. Many members refused to subscribe to the Covenant, our Poet amongst the number, the result being that he was ejected from his Fellowship. His University friends included William Herrys, whose early death he mourned in several Epitaphs; Robert Brook, also the subject of an Epitaph; Robert Shelford; James Staninough, upon whose death he wrote an elegy; and Beaumont, the author of the now well-nigh forgotten poem, *Psyche*, and Abraham Cowley, the Poet. John Selden, of *Table-talk* fame, and the Countess of Denbigh were also of his acquaintance.

Crashaw soon after his ejection seceded from the Protestant Church and retired to France. His friend Cowley, who was in the French capital in 1646, as secretary to Lord Jermyn, found him in great poverty at that time. The Queen of Charles the first was then an exile in Paris, and it is said that Cowley, or Dr. Gough and Mr. Car, introduced our Poet to the Queen, from whom he received letters of recommendation to Italy, where he became secretary at Rome to Cardinal Palotta. He probably remained in Rome until 1650, when, having by his plain speech in regard to certain ecclesiastics made his position an uncomfortable one, he was transferred to the Lady-Chapel of Loretto, of which he was made Canon, by the worthy Cardinal. He died of fever after but a few weeks' residence, and was buried there within the Chapel, in 1650.

One of the finest poetical productions of Cowley was written upon the death of his friend, and with a portion of that melodious utterance we conclude this section of our Introduction. —

"How well (blest Swan) did Fate contrive thy death,
   And made thee render up thy tuneful breath
In thy great Mistress' Arms? Thou most divine
   And richest offering of Loretto's shrine !
Where, like some holy sacrifice t' expire,
   A fever burns thee, and Love lights the fire.
Angels (they say) brought the famed chapel there,
   And bore the sacred load in triumph through the air :
'Tis surer much they brought thee there ; and they,
   And thou, their charge, went singing all the way.

Pardon, my Mother-Church, if I consent
   That Angels led him, when from thee he went ;
For even in error, sure no danger is,
   When joined with so much piety as his. . . . .
His Faith, perhaps, in some nice tenets might
   Be wrong, his Life, I'm sure, was in the right. . . . .
Hail, Bard triumphant ! and some care bestow
   On us, the Poets militant below. . . . .
I ask but half thy mighty spirit for me :
   And when my Muse soars with so strong a wing,
'Twill learn of things divine, and first of thee to sing."

On the Death of Mr. Crashaw.
(COWLEY'S WORKS, 1680 edition, pp. 29-30)

II. CRITICAL.

Although our Poet has never in this nineteenth century been appreciated according to his deserts, by the lover of poetry in general, yet has he not been unjustly neglected by the critics, who, for the most part, have divined his real merits as well as his glaring defects. Possibly the latter have weighed too much against him, and blinded the lover of high and exalted poetry to a perception of Crashaw's qualities and powers, which, in his own age, were almost unique. Among early nineteenth-century critics who have given us estimates of our Poet may be mentioned Samuel Taylor Coleridge, and Robert Aris Willmott. In later time came Dr. George Macdonald's excellent appreciation in *England's Antiphon*, and Dr. Grosart's Essay on the life and poetry, forming the introduction to the second volume of his privately-printed edition of the complete works of Richard Crashaw. Alexander Pope had had his say about our worthy, and even imitated him, his remarks revealing but a limited perception of Crashaw's highest poetical qualities. Pope was just enough to the *letter*, but he failed to recognize the real spirit of Crashaw's poetry. In his enumeration of the "best pieces" of our author he made no mention whatever of such wonderful poems as the *Hymn to S. Teresa*, *To the Name of Jesus*, and several others displaying the highest imagination and spiritual fire. Dr. Johnson evidently did not deem him worthy of a place in his *Lives*; and only once during the eighteenth century was any portion of his works offered to the reading public, viz: in a selection from his English and Latin poems, made by Peregrine Phillips, and published in 1785.

Crashaw's worst defects are his conceits—often outrageous, and highly offensive to good nineteenth-century taste—and his poetic extravagancies, repulsive to the calm and philosophic mind of the thoughtful student of poetry in this our day.

In speaking of the excellences of this Poet we would say that he has an imagination subtle and sweet, a harmony and delicacy of language, a sensuous enjoyment of all good and lofty nature, whether in man, woman, or the outward universe. Combined with these he had the rare and precious poetic gift in a high degree. He is as worthy to be called "the Poet's poet" as is Edmund Spenser. But for the peculiar defects which we have named he would undoubtedly be placed much higher in the hierarchy of Song. He too often let his feelings run away with him, indulging, as we have said, in extravagances of both language and idea, as in *S. Mary Magdalene.* An intense and fiery nature indeed he had, and the lines written by Drayton on Christopher Marlowe will apply equally well to Richard Crashaw.

> "His raptures were
> All air and fire, which made his verses clear;
> For that fine madness still he did retain,
> Which rightly should possess a poet's brain."
> *(Elegies of Poets and Poesy.)*

He even went so far as to exhibit this characteristic in connection with the rites and ceremonies of his dearly-loved Church, regarding the symbol as the person or thing symbolised. He would have been a sensualist had not his Church saved him from the stain. For evidence of this assertion we would refer the reader to the poem addressed to the name of Jesus. His sensuous nature expressed itself in connection with his religious convictions and emotions. In some essential qualities he has affinities to our nineteenth-century poets, Keats and Shelley, possessing the rich imagination and sensuousness of the former, and not a little of the subtlety and music of the latter; and his influence upon more than one nineteenth-century poet of note has been unmistakeable. The subtle and melodious Samuel Taylor Coleridge, referring to certain lines in the *Hymn to S. Teresa*, said "they were ever present to my mind whilst writing the second part of *Christabel*; if, indeed, by some subtle process of the mind, they did not suggest the first thought of the whole poem."—(*Table Talk and Omniana*, ed. by T. Ashe, 1884). Several more recent poets have been similarly influenced by Crashaw, notably Mr. Francis Thompson.

III. BIBLIOGRAPHICAL.

Under this heading we confine ourselves to the enumeration, with occasional remarks, of the various editions of Richard Crashaw's works, from the year 1634 —the date of his first publication—to the present time.

(1) EPIGRAMMATUM SACRORUM LIBER...CANTABRIGIÆ
......1634
(2) STEPS TO THE TEMPLE............LONDON..... 1646
(3) STEPS TO THE TEMPLE......*The 2nd. edition wherein are added divers pieces not before extant.*
LONDON...1648
(4) CARMEN DEO NOSTRO, *Te Decet* Hymnus, Sacred Poems................................... Paris...MDCLII.

† Edited by the poet's friend Thomas Car.
Contains a number of beautiful plates. Copies of this edition are exceedingly rare.

(5) A LETTER FROM MR. CRASHAW TO THE COUNTESS OF DENBIGH...... LONDON [N.D. ? 1653]
(6) STEPS TO THE TEMPLE......The 2nd. [should be 4th.] edition. [London] IN THE SAVOY...1670

† This edition is said to have been reissued, with an undated title page, as "The Third Edition." It is identical in every respect, except the title-page, with this erroneously designated '2nd edition.'

(7) RICHARDI CRASHAWI POEMATA ET EPIGRAMMATA... Editio Secunda, Auctior & emendatior............
CANTABRIGIÆ...1670

† A third edition was issued in 1674, and, save for the title-page, is identical with this issue of 1670.

(8) POETRY, by Richard Crashaw......by Peregrine Phillips. LONDON...1785

† A selection made with a view of giving no offence to Protestant sentiment, consequently lacking the best of Crashaw's sacred verses. It is however a creditable performance for the time.

(9) The Poetical Works of RICHARD CRASHAW.....
(Anderson's "Poets of Great Britain," vol. IV.)
Edinburgh......1793

(10) The Poems of Richard Crashaw (Chalmers' "The Works of the English Poets," vol. VI.) London...1810

(11) The Suspicion of Herod......Trans. from the Italian by Richard Crashaw...... Kensington...1834

(12) The Poetical Works of Richard Crashaw......by Rev. George Gilfillan. (Gilfillan's British Poets) Edinburgh...1857

 † The volume contains Quarles' "Emblems" in addition. The Crashaw text is evidently reprinted from the faulty 1670 edition, repeating all its misprints, &c.

(13) The Complete Works of Richard Crashaw...... Edited by William B. Turnbull, Esq...London...1858

 † One of the volumes of Russell Smith's "Library of Old Authors." Contains the Latin and Greek pieces, which take up half the volume, as well as the English poems. The text is based upon that of 1670, "the most inaccurate of all" (*vide* p. xi) according to the editor of this 1858 edition.

(14) THE FULLER WORTHIES' LIBRARY. THE COMPLETE WORKS OF RICHARD CRASHAW......edited by Rev. Alexander B. Grosart......In two vols. Printed for private circulation. 1872

 † The fullest and best edition yet issued, containing pieces and translations not previously printed. About 300 copies were issued: 50 in quarto, with illustrations; 100 in 8vo; and 150 in 12mo.

(15) POEMS OF RICHARD CRASHAW. Selected and arranged, with notes, by J. R. Tutin. [Motto]

Printed for Private Circulation. 1887. pp. xii & 85.
† 250 copies only were printed, and each copy numbered.

The day is not far distant, we hope, when a complete and scholarly edition of Crashaw will be forthcoming for the readers of this generation. He would be no unworthy addition to any modern series of our British Poets. Along with Herbert, Vaughan, Herrick, Carew, and others of his age—who are well known to modern readers by means of carefully-edited reprints of their works—our 'Poet's poet' deserves an honourable place.

IV. EDITORIAL.

As both title-pages of the present publication indicate, we herein present the reader with a reprint of Crashaw's extremely rare little volume of 1652, a dainty tome published "At Paris" two years after its author's death, and edited by his friend Thomas Car. It is quite evident that this volume was the Poet's own selection from his writings: and on that ground should commend itself to the lover of Richard Crashaw. Car speaks of his authority in connection with the book thus:

"Car was but he that entered as a friend
With whom he shared his thoughts, and did commend
(*While yet he lived*) THIS WORK . . .
So Car hath title then; *'twas his intent*
That what his riches penned, poor Car should print."

It has been our aim to present this noteworthy book in modern orthography, correcting all blunders of the press, of which there are a large number as issued in the volume from the press of Peter Targa. In addition, we have thought well to adopt, in a few cases where the text was palpably erroneous or inferior, the correct, and better versions of some of the poems from the author's own editions of 1646 or 1648. In the case of the lovely poem, *The Weeper* (*St. Mary Magdalene*) we have followed—as did Dr. Grosart in his edition of Crashaw's Works—the succession of its stanzas as in the edition of 1646. All important variations from, or augmentations to, the text of 1652 (in the main a decided advance upon the texts of the two previous editions) we have noted at the foot of the pages.

In conclusion we have but to express our indebtedness to the editor of "The Fuller Worthies' Library," whose edition of Crashaw's entire works has been of not a little service to us, especially in connection with the text of our author.

J. R. TUTIN.

Hull, September 20th, 1897.

Contents.

	PAGE
INTRODUCTION.	v
ORIGINAL TITLE-PAGE.	xix
Crashawe: The Anagram, 'He was Car.'	1
An Epigram upon the Pictures	3
TO THE NOBLEST AND BEST OF LADIES, THE COUNTESS OF DENBIGH	4
TO THE NAME ABOVE EVERY NAME, THE NAME OF JESUS: A HYMN	6
IN THE HOLY NATIVITY OF OUR LORD GOD: A HYMN SUNG AS BY THE SHEPHERDS	15
NEW YEAR'S DAY	20
IN THE GLORIOUS EPIPHANY OF OUR LORD GOD: A HYMN SUNG AS BY THE THREE KINGS	22
TO THE QUEEN'S MAJESTY	32
THE OFFICE OF THE HOLY CROSS:	33
THE HOURS: For the Hour of Matins	33
For the Hour of Prime	34
The Third	36
The Sixth	38
The Ninth	40
Even-Song	42
Compline	44
The Recommendation	45
UPON THE HOLY SEPULCHRE	46
VEXILLA REGIS: THE HYMN OF THE HOLY CROSS	46
TO OUR BLESSED LORD UPON THE CHOICE OF HIS SEPULCHRE	48

CONTENTS.

Charitas Nimia, or the Dear Bargain	49
Sancta Maria Dolorum: or the Mother of Sorrows; A Pathetical descant upon the Devout Plainsong of Stabat Mater Dolorosa	52
Upon the Bleeding Crucifix: A Song	57
Upon the Crown of Thorns taken down from the Head of Our Blessed Lord	59
Upon the Body of Our Blessed Lord	60
The Hymn of St. Thomas in Adoration of the Blessed Sacrament	60
Lauda Sion Salvatorem: The Hymn for the Blessed Sacrament	63
Dies Irae, Dies Illa: The Hymn of the Church in Meditation of the Day of Judgment	67
S. Maria Major: The Hymn, O Gloriosa Domina	70
In the Glorious Assumption of Our Blessed Lady	72
Saint Mary Magdalene, or the Weeper	75
A Hymn to the Name and Honour of the Admirable Saint Teresa	85
An Apology for the foregoing Hymn	92
The Flaming Heart: Upon the Book and Picture of the Seraphical Saint Teresa, as she is usually expressed with a Seraphim beside her	94
A Song: ("Lord, when the sense of Thy sweet Grace.")	98
Prayer: An Ode, which was prefixed to a little Prayer-book given to a young Gentlewoman	99
To the Same Party: Counsel concerning her Choice	103
Alexias: The Complaint of the Forsaken Wife of S. Alexis	
(Three elegies): The First Elegy	106
The Second Elegy	107
The Third Elegy	108
Description of a Religious House and Condition of Life (Out of Barclay)	111

CONTENTS.

AN EPITAPH UPON A YOUNG MARRIED COUPLE DEAD AND BURIED TOGETHER	112
DEATH'S LECTURE AND THE FUNERAL OF A YOUNG GENTLEMAN	113
TEMPERANCE. OF THE CHEAP PHYSICIAN	115
HOPE. [By Cowley]	117
M. CRASHAW'S ANSWER FOR HOPE	118
GLOSSARY	121
INDEX TO THE FIRST LINES	123

CARMEN DEO NOSTRO,

Te Decet Hymnus:

Sacred Poems.

Collected,
Corrected,
Augmented,
Most humbly Presented
To
My Lady
The Countsse [*sic*] of
DENBIGH
By
Her most devoted Servant
R. C.
In heaty [*sic*] acknowledgment of his immortall
obligation to her Goodnes & Charity.

AT PARIS,
By Peter Targa, Printer to the Archbishope ef [*sic*] Paris, in S. Victors streete at the golden sunne.
M. DC. LII.

Carmen deo Nostro.

1. Crashawe,

THE ANAGRAM, 'HE WAS CAR.'

Was Car then Crashawe; or was Crashawe Car,
Since both within one name combinèd are?
Yes, Car's Crashawe, he Car; 'tis love alone
Which melts two hearts, of both composing one.
So Crashawe's still the same—so much desired
By strongest wits, so honour'd, so admired;
Car was but he that enter'd as a friend,
With whom he shared his thoughts, and did commend
(While yet he lived) this work; they loved each other:
Sweet Crashawe was his friend; he Crashawe's brother.
So Car hath title then; 'twas his intent
That what his riches penn'd, poor Car should print;
Nor fears he check, praising that happy one
Who was beloved by all, dispraised by none.
To wit, being pleased with all things, he pleased all;
Nor would he give, nor take offence; befall
What might, he would possess himself, and live
As dead (devoid of int'rest) t' all might give
Dis-ease t' his well-composèd mind, forestall'd

With heavenly riches, which had wholly call'd
His thoughts from earth, to live above in th' air,
A very bird of Paradise.   No care
Had he of earthly trash.   What might suffice
To fit his soul for heavenly exercise
Sufficed him ; and, may we guess his heart
By what his lips bring forth, his only part
Is God and godly thoughts.   Leaves doubt to none
But that to whom one God is all ; all's one.
What he might eat or wear he took no thought ;
His needful food he rather found than sought.
He seeks no downs, no sheets, his bed's still made ;
If he can find a chair or stool, he's laid ;
When Day peeps in, he quits his restless rest,
And still, poor soul, before he's up he's drest.
Thus dying did he live, yet lived to die
In th' Virgin's lap, to whom he did apply
His virgin thoughts and words, and thence was styled
By foes, the chaplain of the Virgin mild,
While yet he lived without.   His modesty
Imparted this to some, and they to me.
Live happy then, dear soul ! enjoy the rest
Eternally by pains thou purchasedst,
While Car must live in care, who was thy friend ;
Nor cares he how he live, so in the end
He may enjoy his dearest Lord and thee,
And sit and sing more skilful songs eternally.

THOMAS CAR.

11. An Epigram.

Upon the Pictures* in the following Poems, which the Author first made with his own hand, admirably well, as may be seen in his Manuscript, dedicated to the Right Honourable Lady the L. Denbigh.

'Twixt pen and pencil rose a holy strife
Which might draw Virtue better to the life:
Best wits gave votes to that, but painters swore
They never saw pieces so sweet before
As these fruits of pure Nature; where no Art
Did lead the untaught pencil, nor had part
In th' work . . . . . .
The hand grown bold, with wit will needs contest:
Doth it prevail? ah, no! say each is best.
This to the ear speaks wonders; that will try
To speak the same, yet louder, to the eye.
Both in their aims are holy, both conspire
To wound, to burn the heart with heavenly fire,
This then's the doom, to do both parties right;
This to the ear speaks best; that, to the sight.

THOMAS CAR.

* This Epigram being portion of the original book, we reprint it in its place although the 'Pictures' of the 1652 volume are not here reproduced.—*Ed.*

To the Noblest and Best of Ladies, the Countess of Denbigh,

PERSUADING HER TO RESOLUTION IN RELIGION, AND TO RENDER HERSELF WITHOUT FURTHER DELAY INTO THE COMMUNION OF THE CATHOLIC CHURCH.

WHAT Heaven-entreated heart is this,
    Stands trembling at the gate of bliss?
Holds fast the door, yet dares not venture
Fairly to open it, and enter;
Whose definition is a doubt
'Twixt life and death, 'twixt in and out.
Say, ling'ring Fair! why comes the birth
Of your brave soul so slowly forth?
Plead your pretences (O you strong
In weakness!) why you choose so long
In labour of yourself to lie,
Nor daring quite to live nor die.
Ah! linger not, loved soul! a slow
And late consent was a long no;
Who grants at last, long time tried
And did his best to have denied:
What magic bolts, what mystic bars,
Maintain the will in these strange wars?
What fatal yet fantastic bands
Keep the free heart from its own hands?
So when the year takes cold, we see
Poor waters their own prisoners be,

Fettered, and lockèd up they lie
In a sad self-captivity.
The astonish'd Nymphs their flood's strange fate deplore,
To see themselves their own severer shore.
Thou that alone canst thaw this cold,
And fetch the heart from its stronghold;
Almighty Love! end this long war,
And of a meteor make a star.
O fix this fair Indefinite!
And 'mongst Thy shafts of sov'reign light
Choose out that sure decisive dart
Which has the key of this close heart,
Knows all the corners of 't, and can control
The self-shut cabinet of an unsearch'd soul.
O let it be at last, Love's hour;
Raise this tall trophy of Thy power;
Come once the conquering way; not to confute
But kill this rebel-word 'irresolute,'
That so, in spite of all this peevish strength
Of weakness, she may write 'resolved' at length.
Unfold at length, unfold fair flower,
And use the season of Love's shower!
Meet His well-meaning wounds, wise heart!
And haste to drink the wholesome dart.
That healing shaft, which Heaven till now
Hath in love's quiver hid for you.
O dart of Love! arrow of light!
O happy you, if it hit right!

It must not fall in vain, it must
Not mark the dry regardless dust.
Fair one, it is your fate ; and brings
Eternal words upon its wings.
Meet it with wide-spread arms, and see
Its seat your soul's just centre be.
Disband dull fears, give faith the day :
To save your life, kill your delay.
It is Love's seige, and sure to be
Your triumph, though His victory.
'Tis cowardice that keeps this field,
And want of courage not to yield.
Yield then, O yield, that Love may win
The fort at last, and let life in.
Yield quickly, lest perhaps you prove
Death's prey, before the prize of Love.
This fort of your fair self, if 't be not won,
He is repulsed indeed, but you're undone.

—:o:—

To the Name above every Name, the Name of Jesus :

A HYMN.

I SING the name which none can say
   But touch'd with an interior ray :
The name of our new peace ; our good :
Our bliss : and supernatural blood :

TO THE NAME OF JESUS.

The name of all our lives and loves.
Hearken, and help, ye holy doves!
The high-born brood of Day; you bright
Candidates of blissful light,
The heirs elect of Love, whose names belong
Unto the everlasting life of song;
All ye wise souls, who in the wealthy breast
Of this unbounded name, build your warm nest.
Awake, my glory, Soul, (if such thou be,
And that fair word at all refer to thee),
  Awake and sing,
  And be all wing;
Bring hither thy whole self; and let me see
What of thy parent Heaven yet speaks in thee.
  O thou art poor
  Of noble powers, I see,
And full of nothing else but empty me:
Narrow, and low, and infinitely less
Than this great morning's mighty business.
  One little world or two
  (Alas!) will never do;
  We must have store.
Go, Soul, out of thyself, and seek for more.
  Go and request
Great Nature for the key of her huge chest
Of Heavens, the self-involving set of spheres
(Which dull mortality more feels than hears).
  Then rouse the nest

Of nimble Art, and traverse round
The airy shop of soul-appeasing sound:
And beat a summons in the same
    All-sovereign name,
To warn each several kind
And shape of sweetness, be they such
    As sigh with supple wind
    Or answer artful touch;
That they convene and come away
To wait at the love-crowned doors of this illustrious day.
Shall we dare this, my Soul? we'll do 't and bring
No other note for 't, but the name we sing.
Wake lute and harp, and every sweet-lipped thing
    That talks with tuneful string;
Start into life, and leap with me
Into a hasty fit-tuned harmony.
    Nor must you think it much
    T' obey my bolder touch;
I have authority in Love's name to take you,
And to the work of Love this morning wake you.
    Wake, in the name
Of Him Who never sleeps, all things that are,
    Or, what's the same,
    Are musical;
    Answer my call
    And come along;
Help me to meditate mine immortal song.
Come, ye soft ministers of sweet sad mirth,

Bring all your household-stuff of Heaven on earth ;
O you, my Soul's most certain wings,
Complaining pipes, and prattling strings,
  Bring all the store
Of sweets you have ; and murmur that you have no more.
  Come, ne'er to part,
  Nature and Art !
  Come ; and come strong,
To the conspiracy of our spacious song.
  Bring all the powers of praise,
Your provinces of well-united worlds can raise :
Bring all your lutes and harps of Heaven and Earth ;
Whate'er co-operates to the common mirth :
  Vessels of vocal joys,
Or you, more noble architects of intellectual noise,
Cymbals of Heaven, or human spheres,
Solicitors of souls or ears ;
  And when you are come, with all
That you can bring or we can call :
  O may you fix
  For ever here, and mix
  Yourselves into the long
And everlasting series of a deathless song ;
Mix all your many worlds above,
And loose them into one of love.
  Cheer thee my heart !
  For thou too hast thy part
  And place in the Great Throng

Of this unbounded all-embracing song.
  Powers of my soul, be proud!
  And speak loud
To all the dear-bought Nations this redeeming Name,
And in the wealth of one rich word, proclaim
New similes to Nature. May it be no wrong,
Blest Heavens, to you and your superior song,
That we, dark sons of dust and sorrow,
  A while dare borrow
The name of your delights, and our desires,
And fit it to so far inferior lyres.
Our murmurs have their music too,
Ye mighty Orbs, as well as you;
  Nor yields the noblest nest
Of warbling Seraphim to the ears of Love,
A choicer lesson than the joyful breast
  Of a poor panting turtle-dove.
And we, low worms, have leave to do
The same bright business (ye Third Heavens) with you.
Gentle spirits, do not complain!
  We will have care
  To keep it fair,
And send it back to you again.
Come, lovely Name! Appear from forth the bright
  Regions of peaceful light;
Look from Thine Own illustrious home,
Fair King of names, and come:
Leave all Thy native glories in their gorgeous nest,

And give Thy Self a while the gracious Guest
Of humble souls, that seek to find
    The hidden sweets
    Which man's heart meets
When Thou art Master of the mind.
Come lovely Name; Life of our hope!
Lo, we hold our hearts wide ope!
Unlock Thy cabinet of Day,
Dearest Sweet, and come away.
    Lo, how the thirsty lands
Gasp for Thy golden showers! with long-stretch'd hands.
    Lo, how the labouring Earth
    That hopes to be
    All Heaven by Thee,
    Leaps at Thy birth!
The attending World, to wait Thy rise,
    First turn'd to eyes;
And then, not knowing what to do,
'Turn'd them to tears, and spent them too.
Come royal Name; and pay the expense
Of all this precious patience;
    O come away
And kill the death of this delay!
O see so many worlds of barren years
Melted and measured out in seas of tears:
O see the weary lids of wakeful Hope
(Love's eastern windows) all wide ope
    With curtain's drawn,

To catch the day-break of Thy dawn.
O dawn at last, long-look'd for Day!
Take Thine own wings and come away.
Lo, where aloft it comes! It comes, among
The conduct of adoring spirits, that throng
Like diligent bees, and swarm about it.
  O they are wise,
And know what sweets are suck'd from out it :
  It is the hive,
  By which they thrive,
Where all their hoard of honey lies.
Lo, where it comes, upon the snowy Dove's
Soft back ; and brings a bosom big with loves ;
Welcome to our dark world, Thou womb of Day!
Unfold Thy fair conceptions, and display
The birth of our bright joys, O Thou compacted
Body of blessings: Spirit of souls extracted!
O dissipate Thy spicy powers,
(Cloud of condensèd sweets) and break upon us
  In balmy showers!
O fill our senses, and take from us all force of so profane
  a fallacy,
To think ought sweet but that which smells of Thee!
Fair, flowery Name, in none but Thee
And Thy nectareal fragrancy,
  Hourly there meets
An universal synod of all sweets ;
By whom it is definèd thus,

That no perfume
For ever shall presume
To pass for odoriferous,
But such alone whose sacred pedigree
Can prove itself some kin (sweet Name!) to Thee.
Sweet Name, in Thy each syllable
A thousand blest Arabias dwell;
A thousand hills of frankincense;
Mountains of myrrh, and beds of spices
And ten thousand Paradises,
The soul that tastes Thee takes from thence.
How many unknown worlds there are
Of comforts, which Thou hast in keeping!
How many thousand mercies there
In Pity's soft lap lie a-sleeping!
Happy he who has the art
To awake them,
And to take them
Home, and lodge them in his heart.
O that it were as it was wont to be!
When Thy old friends of fire, all full of Thee,
Fought against frowns with smiles; gave glorious chase
To persecutions; and against the face
Of Death and fiercest dangers, durst with brave
And sober pace, march on to meet A GRAVE
On their bold breasts, about the world they bore Thee,
And to the teeth of Hell stood up to teach Thee,
In centre of their inmost souls, they wore Thee;

Where racks and torments strived, in vain, to reach Thee.
    Little, alas thought they
Who tore the fair breasts of Thy friends,
    Their fury but made way
For Thee, and served them in Thy glorious ends.
What did their weapons but with wider pores
Enlarge Thy flaming-breasted lovers,
    More freely to transpire
    That impatient fire,
The heart that hides Thee hardly covers?
What did their weapons but set wide the doors
For Thee? fair, purple doors, of Love's devising;
The ruby windows which enrich'd the East
Of Thy so oft-repeated rising!
Each wound of theirs was Thy new morning,
And re-enthroned Thee in Thy rosy nest,
With blush of Thine Own blood Thy day adorning:
It was the wit of Love o'erflow'd the bounds
Of Wrath, and made Thee way through all those wounds.
Welcome, dear, all-adorèd Name!
    For sure there is no knee
    That knows not Thee:
Or, if there be such sons of shame,
    Alas! what will they do
When stubborn rocks shall bow
And hills hang down their heaven-saluting heads
    To seek for humble beds
Of dust, where in the bashful shades of Night

Next to their own low Nothing, they may lie,
And couch before the dazzling light of Thy dread majesty.
They that by Love's mild dictate now
    Will not adore Thee,
Shall then, with just confusion bow
    And break before Thee.

—:o:—

In the Holy Nativity of our Lord God:
A Hymn sung as by the Shepherds.

The Hymn.

Chorus.

COME, we shepherds, whose blest sight
    Hath met Love's noon in Nature's night;
Come, lift we up our loftier song,
And wake the sun that lies too long.

    To all our world of well-stolen joy
He slept; and dreamt of no such thing.
    While we found out Heaven's fairer eye,
And kissed the cradle of our King.
    Tell Him he rises now, too late
To show us aught worth looking at.

    Tell him we now can show him more
Than he e'er show'd to mortal sight;
    Than he himself e'er saw before,
Which to be seen needs not his light.

Tell him, Tityrus, where th' hast been,
Tell him, Thyrsis, what th' hast seen.

TITYRUS.

Gloomy night embraced the place
Where the noble Infant lay.
   The Babe looked up and showed His face;
In spite of darkness, it was day.
   It was Thy day, Sweet! and did rise,
Not from the East, but from Thine eyes.
      Chorus.—It was Thy day, Sweet.

THYRSIS.

Winter chid aloud, and sent
The angry North to wage his wars.
   The North forgot his fierce intent,
And left perfumes instead of scars.
   By those sweet eyes' persuasive powers,
Where he meant frost, he scattered flowers.
      Chorus.—By those sweet eyes'.

BOTH.

We saw Thee in Thy balmy-nest,
Young dawn of our eternal Day!
   We saw Thine eyes break from their East,
And chase the trembling shades away.
   We saw Thee; and we blest the sight,
We saw Thee by Thine Own sweet light.

TITYRUS.
Poor world (said I), what wilt thou do
To entertain this starry Stranger?
  Is this the best thou canst bestow?
A cold, and not too cleanly, manger?
  Contend, the powers of Heaven and Earth,
To fit a bed for this huge birth?
    Chorus.—Contend, the powers.

THYRSIS.
Proud world, said I, cease your contest,
And let the mighty Babe alone.
  The phœnix builds the phœnix' nest,
Love's architecture is his own.
  The Babe whose birth embraves this morn,
Made His Own bed ere He was born.
    Chorus.—The Babe whose.

TITYRUS.
I saw the curled drops, soft and slow,
Come hovering o'er the place's head;
  Offering their whitest sheets of snow
To furnish the fair Infant's bed:
  Forbear, said I; be not too bold,
Your fleece is white, but 'tis too cold.
    Chorus.—Forbear, said I.

THYRSIS.
I saw the obsequious Seraphims
Their rosy fleece of fire bestow,

For well they now can spare their wing,
Since Heaven itself lies here below.
   Well done, said I; but are you sure
Your down so warm, will pass for pure?
      Chorus.—Well done, said I.

TITYRUS.

No, no! your King's not yet to seek
Where to repose His royal head;
   See, see, how soon His new-bloom'd cheek
'Twixt 's mother's breasts is gone to bed.
   Sweet choice, said we! no way but so
Not to lie cold, yet sleep in snow.
      Chorus.—Sweet choice, said we.

BOTH.

We saw Thee in Thy balmy nest,
Bright dawn of our eternal Day!
   We saw Thine eyes break from their East,
And chase the trembling shades away.
   We saw Thee: and we blest the sight,
We saw Thee by Thine Own sweet light.
      Chorus.—We saw Thee, &c.

FULL CHORUS.

Welcome, all wonders in one sight!
Eternity shut in a span!
   Summer in Winter, Day in Night!
Heaven in Earth, and God in man!

IN THE HOLY NATIVITY.

Great, little One! whose all-embracing birth
Lifts Earth to Heaven, stoops Heaven to Earth.
  Welcome, though not to gold nor silk,
To more than Cæsar's birthright is;
  Two sister-seas of virgin-milk,
With many a rarely-temper'd kiss,
  That breathes at once both maid and mother,
Warms in the one, cools in the other.
  She sings Thy tears asleep, and dips
Her kisses in Thy weeping eye;
  She spreads the red leaves of Thy lips,
That in their buds yet blushing lie:
  She 'gainst those mother-diamonds, tries
The points of her young eagle's eyes.
  Welcome, though not to those gay flies,
Gilded i' th' beams of earthly kings;
  Slippery souls in smiling eyes:
But to poor shepherds' home-spun things;
  Whose wealth's their flock; whose wit, to be
Well-read in their simplicity.
  Yet when young April's husband-showers
Shall bless the fruitful Maia's bed,
  We'll bring the first-born of her flowers
To kiss Thy feet, and crown Thy head.
  To Thee, dread Lamb! Whose love must keep
The shepherds, more than they the sheep.
  To Thee, meek Majesty! soft King
Of simple Graces and sweet Loves:

Each of us his lamb will bring,
Each his pair of silver doves:
 Till burnt at last in fire of Thy fair eyes,
Ourselves become our own best sacrifice.

—:o:—

New Year's Day.

RISE, thou best and brightest morning!
   Rosy with a double red;
With thine own blush thy cheeks adorning,
   And the dear drops this day were shed.

All the purple pride, that laces
   The crimson curtains of thy bed,
Gilds thee not with so sweet graces,
   Nor sets thee in so rich a red.

Of all the fair-cheek'd flowers that fill thee,
   None so fair thy bosom strows,
As this modest maiden lily
   Our sins have shamed into a rose.

Bid thy golden god, the sun,
   Burnish'd in his best beams rise,
Put all his red-eyed rubies on;
   These rubies shall put out their eyes.

Let him make poor the purple East,
   Search what the world's close cabinets keep,

NEW YEAR'S DAY.

Rob the rich births of each bright nest
    That flaming in their fair beds sleep.

Let him embrave his own bright tresses
    With a new morning made of gems;
And wear, in those his wealthy dresses,
    Another day of diadems.

When he hath done all he may,
    To make himself rich in his rise,
All will be darkness to the day
    That breaks from one of these bright eyes.

And soon this sweet truth shall appear,
    Dear Babe, ere many days be done:
The Morn shall come to meet Thee here,
    And leave her own neglected sun.

Here are beauties shall bereave him
    Of all his eastern paramours:
His Persian lovers all shall leave him,
    And swear faith to Thy sweeter powers.

In the Glorious Epiphany of our Lord God:

A HYMN SUNG AS BY THE THREE KINGS.

1 King—BRIGHT Babe, Whose awful beauties make
    The morn incur a sweet mistake;
2 King—For Whom the officious Heavens devise
    To disinherit the sun's rise:
3 King—Delicately to displace
    The day, and plant it fairer in Thy face;
1 King—O Thou born King of loves,
2 King—Of lights,
3 King—Of joys.
Chorus—Look up, sweet Babe, look up, and see
    For love of Thee
    Thus far from home
    The East is come
    To seek herself in Thy sweet eyes.
1 King—We, who strangely went astray,
    Lost in a bright
    Meridian night,
2 King—A darkness made of too much day.
3 King—Beckon'd from far
    By Thy fair star,
    Lo, at last have found our way.

Chorus—To Thee, thou Day of Night! thou East of West!
    Lo, we at last have found the way
    To Thee the World's great universal East,
    The general and indifferent Day.

1 King— All-circling point ! all-centring sphere !
  The World's one, round, eternal year.
2 King— Whose full and all-unwrinkled face
  Nor sinks nor swells with time or place ;
3 King— But every where, and every while
  Is one consistent, solid smile.
1 King— Not vex'd and tost
2 King— Twixt Spring and frost,
3 King— Nor by alternate shreds of light,
  Sordidly shifting hands with shades and Night.

Chorus— O little all ! in Thy embrace
  The World lies warm, and likes his place ;
  Nor does his full globe fail to be
  Kiss'd on both his cheeks by Thee :
  Time is too narrow for Thy year,
  Nor makes the whole World Thy half-sphere.

1 King— To Thee, to Thee
   From him we flee.
2 King— From him, whom by a more illustrious lie,
  The blindness of the World did call the eye.
3 King— To Him, Who by these mortal clouds hast made
  Thyself our sun, though Thine Own shade.
2 King— Farewell, the World's false light !
   Farewell, the white
    Egypt, a long farewell to thee,
   Bright idol, black idolatry :
  The dire face of inferior darkness, kist

And courted in the pompous mask of a more
    specious mist.

2 King—   Farewell, farewell
The proud and misplaced gates of hell,
Perch'd in the Morning's way,
And double-gilded as the doors of Day:
The deep hypocrisy of Death and Night
More desperately dark, because more bright.

3 King—   Welcome, the World's sure way!
Heaven's wholesome ray.

Chorus—   Welcome to us; and we
(Sweet!) to ourselves, in Thee.

*1 King—*The deathless Heir of all Thy Father's day;
2 King—   Decently born!
Embosom'd in a much more rosy Morn:
The blushes of Thy all-unblemish'd mother,
3 King—   No more that other
Aurora shall set ope
Her ruby casements, or hereafter hope
From mortal eyes
To meet religious welcomes at her rise.

*Chorus—*We (precious ones!) in you have won
A gentler Morn, a juster sun.

*1 King—*His superficial beams sun-burnt our skin;
2 King—   But left within
*3 King—*The Night and Winter still of Death and Sin.

Chorus—Thy softer yet more certain darts
   Spare our eyes, but pierce our hearts:
1 King—Therefore with his proud Persian spoils
2 King—We court Thy more concerning smiles.
3 King—   Therefore with his disgrace
   We gild the humble cheek of this chaste place;
Chorus—And at Thy feet pour forth his face.
1 King—The doating Nations now no more
   Shall any day but Thine adore.
2 King—Nor (much less) shall they leave these eyes
   For cheap Egyptian deities.
3 King—In whatsoe'er more sacred shape
   Of ram, he-goat, or rev'rend ape;
   Those beauteous ravishers oppress'd so sore
   The too-hard tempted nations:
1 King—   Never more
   By wanton heifer shall be worn
2 King—A garland, or a gilded horn:
   The altar-stall'd ox, fat Osris now
   With his fair sister cow,
3 King—Shall kick the clouds no more; but lean and tame,
Chorus—See His horn'd face, and die for shame:
   And Mithra now shall be no name.
1 King—No longer shall the immodest lust
   Of adulterous godless dust
2 King—Fly in the face of Heaven; as if it were
   The poor World's fault that He is fair.

3 King—Nor with perverse loves and religious rapes
        Revenge Thy bounties in their beauteous shapes;
        And punish best things worst, because they stood
        Guilty of being much for them too good.
1 King—Proud sons of Death! that durst compel
        Heaven itself to find them Hell:
2 King—And by strange wit of madness wrest
        From this World's East the other's West.
3 King—All-idolizing worms! that thus could crowd
        And urge their sun into Thy cloud;
        Forcing His sometimes eclips'd face to be
        A long deliquium to the light of Thee.

Chorus—Alas! with how much heavier shade
        The shamefaced lamp hung down his head,
            For that one eclipse he made,
            Than all those he suffered!

1 King—For this he looked so big, and ev'ry morn
        With a red face confess'd his scorn;
        Or, hiding his vex'd cheeks in a hired mist,
        Kept them from being so unkindly kist.
2 King—It was for this the Day did rise
            So oft with blubber'd eyes;
        For this the Evening wept; and we ne'er knew,
            But called it dew.
3 King—   This daily wrong
        Silenced the morning sons, and damp'd their
            song.

Chorus—Nor was 't our deafness, but our sins, that thus
　　　　Long made th' harmonious orbs all mute to us.

1 King—　　Time has a day in store
　　　　When this so proudly poor
　　And self-oppressèd spark, that has so long
　　By the love-sick World been made
　　Not so much their sun as shade:
　　Weary of this glorious wrong,
　　From them and from himself shall flee
　　For shelter to the shadow of Thy tree;

Chorus—Proud to have gain'd this precious loss,
　　　　And changed his false crown for Thy cross.

2 King— That dark Day's clear doom shall define
　　Whose is the master Fire, which sun should shine;
　　That sable judgment-seat shall by new laws
　　Decide and settle the great cause
　　　　Of controverted light:

Chorus—And Nature's wrongs rejoice to do Thee right.

3 King—That forfeiture of Noon to Night shall pay
　　All the idolatrous thefts done by this Night of
　　　　Day;
　　And the great Penitent press his own pale lips
　　With an elaborate love-eclipse:
　　　　To which the low World's laws
　　　　Shall lend no cause,

Chorus—Save those domestic which He borrows
　　　　From our sins and His Own sorrows.

1 King—Three sad hours' sackcloth then shall show to us
　　His penance, as our fault, conspicuous :
2 King—And He more needfully and nobly prove
　　The Nations' terror now than erst their love ;
3 King—Their hated love's changed into wholesome fears:
Chorus—The shutting of His eye shall open theirs.

1 King—As by a fair-eyed fallacy of Day
　　Misled, before, they lost their way ;
　　So shall they, by the seasonable fright
　　Of an unseasonable Night,
　　Loosing it once again, stumble on true Light :
2 King—And as before His too-bright eye
　　Was their more blind idolatry ;
　　So his officious blindness now shall be
　　Their black, but faithful perspective of Thee.
3 King—　　His new prodigious Night,
　　Their new and admirable light,
　　The supernatural dawn of Thy pure Day ;
　　　　While wondering they
　　(The happy converts now of Him
　　Whom they compell'd before to be their sin)
　　　　Shall henceforth see
　　To kiss him only as their rod,
　　Whom they so long courted as God.
Chorus—And their best use of him they worshipp'd, be
　　To learn of him at last, to worship Thee.

1 King—It was their weakness woo'd his beauty ;

But it shall be
Their wisdom now, as well as duty,
To enjoy his blot; and as a large black letter
Use it to spell Thy beauties better;
And make the Night itself their torch to Thee.

2 King—By the oblique ambush of this close night
  Couch'd in that conscious shade
The right-eyed Areopagite
Shall with a vigorous guess invade
And catch Thy quick reflex; and sharply see
  On this dark ground
  To descant Thee.

3 King—O prize of the rich Spirit! with what fierce chase
  Of his strong soul, shall he
  Leap at thy lofty face,
And seize the swift flash, in rebound
From this obsequious cloud,
  Once call'd a sun,
  'Till dearly thus undone;

Chorus—Till thus triumphantly tamed (O ye two
  Twin-suns!) and taught now to negotiate you,

1 King—Thus shall that rev'rend child of Light,
2 King—By being scholar first of that new Night,
  Come forth great master of the mystic Day;
3 King—And teach obscure mankind a more close way,
  By the frugal negative light
  Of a most wise and well-abusèd Night,
  To read more legible Thine original ray;

Chorus--And make our darkness serve thy Day;
        Maintaining 'twixt Thy World and ours
        A commerce of contrary powers,
            A mutual trade
            'Twixt sun and shade,
        By confederate black and white
        Borrowing Day and lending Night.

1 King—Thus we, who when with all the noble powers
        That (at Thy cost) are call'd, not vainly, ours:
           We vow to make brave way
        Upwards, and press on for the pure intelligential
          prey;
2 King—   At least to play
           The amorous spies,
        And peep and proffer at Thy sparkling throne;
3 King—Instead of bringing in the blissful prize
           And fastening on Thine eyes:
           Forfeit our own
           And nothing gain
        But more ambitious loss at last, of brain;
Chorus—Now by abasèd lids shall learn to be
        Eagles, and shut our eyes that we may see.

THE CLOSE.

[*Chorus*] -Therefore to Thee and Thine auspicious ray
            (Dread Sweet!) lo thus
            At last by us,

The delegated eye of Day
Does first his sceptre, then himself, in solemn
  tribute pay.
    Thus he undresses
    His sacred unshorn tresses;
  At Thy adorèd feet, thus he lays down
1 King—　　His gorgeous tire
　　　　Of flame and fire,
2 King—His glittering robe, *3 King*—His sparkling crown;
1 King—His gold, *2 King*—His myrrh, *3 King*—His
  frankincense;
Chorus—To which he now has no pretence:
  For being show'd by this Day's light, how far
  He is from sun enough to make Thy star,
  His best ambition now is but to be
  Something a brighter shadow, Sweet, of Thee.
  Or on Heaven's azure forehead high to stand
  Thy golden index; with a duteous hand
  Pointing us home to our own sun,
  The world's and his Hyperion.

To the Queen's Majesty.

MADAM,

'Mongst those long rows of crowns that gild your race,
These royal sages sue for decent place:
The daybreak of the Nations; their first ray,
When the dark World dawn'd into Christian Day,
And smil'd i' th' Babe's bright face: the purpling bud
And rosy dawn of the right royal blood;
Fair first-fruits of the Lamb! sure kings in this,
They took a kingdom while they gave a kiss.
But the World's homage, scarce in these well-blown,
We read in you (rare queen) ripe and full-grown.
For from this day's rich seed of diadems
Does rise a radiant crop of royal stems,
A golden harvest of crown'd heads, that meet
And crowd for kisses from the Lamb's white feet:
In this illustrious throng, your lofty flood
Swells high, fair confluence of all high-born blood:
With your bright head whole groves of sceptres bend
Their wealthy tops, and for these feet contend.
So swore the Lamb's dread Sire, and so we see't,
Crowns, and the heads they kiss, must court these feet.
Fix here, fair majesty! may your heart ne'er miss
To reap new crowns and kingdoms from that kiss;
Nor may we miss the joy to meet in you
The aged honours of this day still new.
May the great time, in you, still greater be,

While all the year is your epiphany ;
While your each day's devotion duly brings
Three kingdoms to supply this day's three kings.

—:o:—

The Office of The Holy Cross.

Tradidit semetipsum pro nobis oblationem et hostiam Deo in odorem suavitatis. *Ad Ephe.*, *v*. 2.

THE HOURS.

For the Hour of Matins.

The Versicle.

Lord, by Thy sweet and saving sign!

The Responsor.

Defend us from our foes and Thine.

V. Thou shalt open my lips, O Lord
R. And my mouth shall shew forth Thy praise.
V. O, God, make speed to save me.
R. O Lord, make haste to help me.
   Glory be to the Father,
      and to the Son,
      and to the H[oly] Ghost.
As it was in the beginning, is now, and ever shall be,
   world without end. *Amen.*

THE HYMN.

The wakeful Matins haste to sing
The unknown sorrows of our King:

The Father's Word and Wisdom, made
Man for man, by man's betray'd ;
The World's price set to sale, and by the bold
Merchants of Death and Sin, is bought and sold:
Of His best friends (yea of Himself) forsaken ;
By His worst foes (because He would) besieged and
    taken.

The Antiphon.

    All hail, fair tree
    Whose fruit we be !
    What song shall raise
    Thy seemly praise,
    Who brought'st to light
Life out of death, Day out of Night !

The Versicle.

Lo, we adore Thee,
Dread LAMB! and bow thus low before Thee:

The Responsor.

'Cause by the covenant of thy cross,
Thou hast saved at once the whole World's loss.

The Prayer.

O Lord JESU-CHRIST, Son of the living God! interpose, I pray Thee, Thine Own precious death, Thy cross and passion, betwixt my soul and Thy judgment, now and in the hour of my death. And vouchsafe to grant unto me Thy grace and mercy; unto all quick and dead, remission and rest ; to Thy Church, peace and concord; to us sinners, life and glory everlasting. Who livest and reignest with the Father, in the unity of the Holy Ghost, one God, world without end. *Amen.*

FOR THE HOUR OF PRIME.

The Versicle.

LORD, by Thy sweet and saving sign!

The Responsor.

Defend us from our foes and Thine.

V. Thou shalt open my lips, O Lord,
R. And my mouth shall shew forth Thy praise.
V. O God, make speed to save me.
R. O Lord, make haste to help me.
V. Glory be to, etc.
R. As it was in the, etc.

THE HYMN.

The early Prime blushes to say
She could not rise so soon, as they
Call'd Pilate up, to try if he
Could lend them any cruelty;
Their hands with lashes arm'd, their tongues with lies,
And loathsome spittle, blot those beauteous eyes,
The blissful springs of joy; from whose all-cheering ray
The fair stars fill their wakeful fires, the sun himself
   drinks day.

The Antiphon.

Victorious sign
That now dost shine,

Transcribed above
Into the land of light and love ;
   O let us twine
   Our roots with thine,
   That we may rise
   Upon Thy wings and reach the skies.

The Versicle.

   Lo, we adore Thee,
Dread Lamb! and fall
   Thus low before Thee.

The Responsor.

'Cause by the covenant of Thy cross
Thou hast saved at once the whole World's loss.

The Prayer.

O Lord JESU CHRIST, Son of the living God! interpose, I pray Thee, Thine Own precious death, Thy cross and passion, betwixt my soul and Thy judgment, now and in the hour of my death. And vouchsafe to grant unto me Thy grace and mercy; unto all quick and dead, remission and rest; to Thy Church, peace and concord; to us sinners, life and glory everlasting. Who livest and reignest with the Father, in the unity of the Holy Ghost, one God, world without end. *Amen.*

THE THIRD.

The Versicle.

LORD, by Thy sweet and saving sign,

THE HOLY CROSS.

The Responsor.

Defend us from our foes and Thine.
- V. Thou shalt open my lips, O, Lord.
- R. And my mouth shall shew forth Thy praise.
- V. O God, make speed to save me.
- R. O Lord, make haste to help me.
- V. Glory be to, etc.
- R. As it was in the, etc.

THE HYMN.

The third hour's deafen'd with the cry
Of 'Crucify Him, crucify.'
So goes the vote (nor ask them, why?)
'Live Barabbas! and let God die.'
But there is wit in wrath, and they will try
A 'Hail' more cruel than their 'Crucify.'
For while in sport He wears a spiteful crown,
The serious showers along His decent Face run sadly down.

The Antiphon.

Christ when He died
Deceived the Cross;
And on Death's side
Threw all the loss.
The captive World awaked and found
The prisoner loose, the jailor bound.

The Versicle.

Lo, we adore Thee,
Dread LAMB! and fall
Thus low before Thee.

The Responsor.

'Cause by the covenant of Thy cross
Thou hast saved at once the whole World's loss.

The Prayer.

O Lord JESU-CHRIST, Son of the living God! interpose, I pray Thee, Thine Own precious death, Thy cross and passion, betwixt my soul and Thy judgment, now and in the hour of my death. And vouchsafe to grant unto me Thy grace and mercy : unto all quick and dead, remission and rest ; to Thy Church, peace and concord ; to us sinners, life and glory everlasting. Who livest and reignest with the Father, in the unity of the Holy Ghost, one God, world without end. Amen.

THE SIXTH.

The Versicle.

LORD, by Thy sweet and saving sign,

The Responsor.

Defend us from our foes and Thine.

V. Thou shalt open my lips, O Lord,

R. And my mouth shall shew forth Thy praise.

V. O God, make speed to save me!

R. O Lord, make haste to help me!
V. Glory be to, etc.
R. As it was in the, etc.

THE HYMN.

Now is the noon of Sorrows night:
High in His patience, as their spite,
Lo, the faint Lamb, with weary limb
Bears that huge tree which must bear Him.
The fatal plant, so great of fame,
For fruit of sorrow and of shame,
Shall swell with both, for Him; and mix
All woes into one crucifix.
Is tortured thirst itself too sweet a cup?
Gall, and more bitter mocks, shall make it up.
Are nails blunt pens of superficial smart?
Contempt and scorn can send sure wounds to search the inmost heart.

The Antiphon.

O dear and sweet dispute
'Twixt Death's and Love's far different fruit!
Different as far
As antidotes and poisons are
By that first fatal tree
Both life and liberty
Were sold and slain;
By this they both look up, and live again.

The Versicle.

Lo, we adore Thee,
Dread Lamb! and bow thus low before Thee.

The Responsor.

'Cause by the covenant of Thy cross,
Thou hast saved the World from certain loss.

The Prayer.

O Lord Jesu-Christ, Son of the living God! interpose, I pray Thee, Thine Own precious death, Thy cross and passion, betwixt my soul and Thy judgment, now and in the hour of my death. And vouchsafe to grant unto me Thy grace and mercy; unto all quick and dead, remission and rest; to Thy Church, peace and concord; to us sinners, life and glory everlasting. Who livest and reignest with the Father, in the unity of the Holy Ghost, One God, world without end. Amen.

THE NINTH.

The Versicle.

Lord, by Thy sweet and saving sign,

The Responsor.

Defend us from our foes and Thine.

V. Thou shalt open my lips, O Lord,
R. And my mouth shall shew forth Thy praise.
V. O God, make speed to save me!
R. O Lord, make haste to help me!
V. Glory be to, etc.
R. As it was in the, etc.

THE HYMN.

The ninth with awful horror hearkened to those groans
Which taught attention even to rocks and stones.
Hear, Father, hear! thy Lamb (at last) complains
Of some more painful thing than all His pains.
Then bows His all-obedient head, and dies
His own love's, and our sins' GREAT SACRIFICE.
The sun saw that, and would have seen no more;
The centre shook: her useless veil th' inglorious Temple
    tore!

The Antiphon.

O strange, mysterious strife
Of open Death and hidden Life!
When on the cross my King did bleed,
Life seem'd to die, Death died indeed.

The Versicle.

Lo, we adore Thee,
Dear Lamb! and fall
Thus low before Thee.

The Responsor.

'Cause by the covenant of Thy cross,
Thou hast saved at once the whole World's loss.

The Prayer.

O Lord JESU-CHRIST, Son of the living God! interpose, I pray Thee, Thine Own precious death, Thy cross and passion, betwixt my soul and Thy judgment, now and in the hour of my death. And vouchsafe to grant unto me Thy grace and mercy: unto all quick and dead, remission and rest; to Thy Church, peace and concord; to us sinners, life and glory everlasting. Who livest and reignest with the Father, in the unity of the Holy Ghost, one God, world without end. *Amen.*

EVEN-SONG.

The Versicle.

LORD, by Thy sweet and saving sign!

The Responsor.

Defend us from our foes and Thine.

V. Thou shalt open my lips, O Lord!
R. And my mouth shall shew forth Thy praise.
V. O God, make speed to save me!
R. O Lord, make haste to help me!
V. Glory be to, etc.
R. As it was in the, etc.

THE HYMN.

But there were rocks would not relent at this:
Lo, for their own hearts, they rend His;
Their deadly hate lives still, and hath
A wild reserve of wanton wrath;
Superfluous spear! But there's a heart stands by
Will look no wounds be lost, no death shall die.
Gather now thy Grief's ripe fruit, great mother-maid!
Then sit thee down, and sing thine even-song in the sad
    tree's shade.

THE HOLY CROSS.

The Antiphon.

O sad, sweet tree!
Woeful and joyful we
Both weep and sing in shade of thee.
When the dear nails did lock
And graft into thy gracious stock
　　The hope, the health,
　　The worth, the wealth
Of all the ransomed World, thou hadst the power
　　(In that propitious hour)
　　To poise each precious limb,
And prove how light the World was, when it weighed
　　with Him.
　　　Wide mayest thou spread
Thine arms, and with thy bright and blissful head
O'erlook all Libanus. Thy lofty crown
The King Himself is; thou His humble throne,
Where yielding and yet conquering He
Proved a new path of patient victory:
When Wondering Death by death was slain,
And our Captivity His captive ta'en.

The Versicle.

Lo, we adore Thee,
Dread LAMB! and bow thus low before Thee.

The Responsor.

'Cause by the covenant of Thy cross,
Thou hast saved the World from certain loss.

The Prayer.

O Lord Jesu Christ, Son of the living, etc.

COMPLINE.

The Versicle.

Lord, by Thy sweet and saving sign!

The Responsor.

Defend us from our foes and Thine.
V. Thou shalt open my lips, O Lord
R. And my mouth shall shew forth Thy praise.
V. O God, make speed to save me!
R. O Lord, make haste to help me!
V. Glory be to, &c.
R. As it was in the, &c.

THE HYMN.

The Complin hour comes last, to call
Us to our own lives' funeral.
Ah, heartless task! yet Hope takes head,
And lives in Him that here lies dead.
Run, Mary, run! bring hither all the blest
Arabia, for thy royal phœnix' nest;
Pour on thy noblest sweets, which, when they touch
This sweeter body, shall indeed be such.
But must Thy bed, Lord, be a borrowed grave,
Who lend'st to all things all the life they have?
O rather use this heart, thus far a fitter stone,

'Cause, though a hard and cold one, yet it is Thine own.
Amen.

The Antiphon.

O save us then,
Merciful King of men!
Since Thou wouldst needs be thus
A Saviour, and at such a rate, for us;
Save us, O save us, Lord.
We now will own no shorter wish, nor name a
narrower word;
Thy blood bids us be bold,
Thy wounds give us fair hold,
Thy sorrows chide our shame:
Thy cross, Thy nature, and Thy name
Advance our claim,
And cry with one accord,
Save them, O save them, Lord!

THE RECOMMENDATION.

These hours, and that which hovers o'er my end,
Into Thy hands and heart, Lord, I commend.

Take both to Thine account, that I and mine,
In that hour and in these, may be all Thine.

That as I dedicate my devoutest breath
To make a kind of life for my Lord's death,

So from His living, and life-giving death,
My dying life may draw a new and never fleeting breath,

Upon The Holy Sepulchre

Here, where our Lord once laid his head,
Now the grave lies buried.

— :o:—

Vexilla Regis:
THE HYMN OF THE HOLY CROSS.

I.

Look up, languishing soul! Lo, where the fair
Badge of thy faith calls back thy care,
    And bids thee ne'er forget
    Thy life is one long debt
Of love to Him, Who on this painful tree
Paid back the flesh He took for thee.

II.

Lo, how the streams of life, from that full nest,
Of loves, Thy Lord's too liberal breast,
    Flow in an amorous flood
    Of water wedding blood.
With these He wash'd thy stain, transferr'd thy smart,
And took it home to His own heart.

III.

But though great Love, greedy of such sad gain,
Usurp'd the portion of thy pain,
    And from the nails and spear
    Turn'd the steel point of fear:

Their use is changed, not lost ; and now they move
Not stings of wrath, but wounds of love.

IV.

Tall tree of life ! thy truth makes good
What was till now ne'er understood,
      Though the prophetic king
      Struck loud his faithful string :
It was thy wood he meant should make the throne
For a more than Solomon.

V.

Large throne of Love ! royally spread
With purple of too rich a red :
      Thy crime is too much duty ;
      Thy burthen too much beauty ;
Glorious or grievous more ? thus to make good
Thy costly excellence with thy King's own blood.

VI.

Even balance of both worlds ! our world of sin,
And that of grace, Heaven-way'd in Him :
      Us with our price thou weighedst ;
      Our price for us thou payedst,
Soon as the right-hand scale rejoiced to prove
How much Death weigh'd more light than Love.

VII.

Hail, our alone hope ! let thy fair head shoot
Aloft, and fill the nations with thy noble fruit :

The while our hearts and we
Thus graft ourselves on thee,
Grow thou and they. And be thy fair increase
The sinners pardon and the just man's peace.

VIII.

Live, O for ever live and reign
The Lamb Whom His own love hath slain!
And let Thy lost sheep live to inherit
That kingdom which this Cross did merit. *Amen.*

—:o:—

To Our B. Lord upon the Choice of His Sepulchre.

How life and death in Thee
          Agree!
Thou hadst a virgin womb,
          And tomb.
A Joseph did betroth
          Them both.

Charitas Nimia,

Or, The Dear Bargain.

Lord, what is man? why should he cost Thee
So dear? what had his ruin lost Thee?
Lord, what is man, that thou hast over-bought
So much a thing of nought?

Love is too kind, I see; and can
Make but a simple merchant-man.
'Twas for such sorry merchandise
Bold painters have put out his eyes.

Alas, sweet Lord, what were't to Thee
If there were no such worms as we?
Heaven ne'ertheless still Heaven would be,
  Should mankind dwell
  In the deep Hell:
What have his woes to do with Thee?

  Let him go weep
  O'er his own wounds;
  Seraphims will not sleep,
Nor spheres let fall their faithful rounds.

  Still would the youthful spirits sing;
And still Thy spacious palace ring;
Still would those beauteous ministers of light
  Burn all as bright;
And bow their flaming heads before Thee;

Still thrones and dominations would adore Thee ;
Still would those ever-wakeful sons of fire
    Keep warm Thy praise
    Both nights and days,
And teach Thy loved name to their noble lyre.

Let froward dust then do its kind ;
And give itself for sport to the proud wind.
Why should a piece of peevish clay plead shares
In the eternity of Thy old cares?
Why should'st Thou bow Thy awful breast to see
What mine own madnesses have done with me?

Should not the king still keep his throne
Because some desperate fool's undone?
Or will the World's illustrious eyes
Weep for every worm that dies?

    Will the gallant sun
    E'er the less glorious run ?
Will he hang down his golden head,
Or e'er the sooner seek his Western bed,
    Because some foolish fly
    Grows wanton, and will die?

If I were lost in misery,
What was it to Thy Heaven and Thee ?
What was it to Thy precious blood,
If my foul heart call'd for a flood?

CHARITAS NIMIA.

What if my faithless soul and I
    Would needs fall in
    With guilt and sin ;
What did the Lamb that He should die?
What did the Lamb that He should need,
When the wolf sins, Himself to bleed?

    If my base lust
Bargain'd with Death and well-beseeming dust:
    Why should the white
    Lamb's bosom write
    The purple name
    Of my sin's shame?
Why should His unstain'd breast make good
My blushes with His Own heart-blood?

O my Saviour, make me see
How dearly Thou hast paid for me ;
That lost again, my life may prove,
As then in death, so now in love.

Sancta Maria Dolorum:

OR, THE MOTHER OF SORROWS: A PATHETICAL DESCANT UPON THE DEVOUT PLAINSONG OF STABAT MATER DOLOROSA.

I.

In shade of Death's sad tree
    Stood doleful she.
Ah she! now by none other
Name to be known, alas, but Sorrow's Mother.
    Before her eyes
Her's and the whole World's joys,
Hanging all torn, she sees; and in His woes
And pains, her pangs and throes:
Each wound of His, from every part,
All, more at home in her one heart.

II.

    What kind of marble then
    Is that cold man
    Who can look on and see,
Nor keep such noble sorrows company?
    Sure even from you
    (My flints) some drops are due,
To see so many unkind swords contest
    So fast for one soft breast:
While with a faithful, mutual flood,
Her eyes bleed tears, His wounds weep blood.

III.

    O costly intercourse
    Of deaths, and worse—
Divided loves. While Son and mother
Discourse alternate wounds to one another,
    Quick deaths that grow
    And gather, as they come and go:
His nails write swords in her, which soon her heart
    Pays back, with more than their own smart;
Her swords, still growing with His pain,
Turn spears, and straight come home again.

IV.

    She sees her Son, her God,
    Bow with a load
    Of borrow'd sins; and swim
In woes that were not made for Him.
    Ah! hard command
Of love! Here must she stand,
Charged to look on, and with a steadfast eye
    See her life die;
Leaving her only so much breath
As serves to keep alive her death.

V.

    O mother turtle-dove!
    Soft source of love!
    That these dry lids might borrow
Something from thy full seas of sorrow!

O in that breast
Of thine (the noblest nest
Both of Love's fires and floods) might I recline
This hard, cold heart of mine!
The chill lump would relent, and prove
Soft subject for the siege of Love.

VI.

O teach those wounds to bleed
In me; me, so to read
This book of loves, thus writ
In lines of death, my life may copy it
With loyal cares.
O let me, here, claim shares!
Yield something in thy sad prerogative
(Great queen of griefs!), and give
Me, too, my tears; who, though all stone,
Think much that thou shouldst mourn alone.

VII.

Yea, let my life and me
Fix here with thee,
And at the humble foot
Of this fair tree, take our eternal root.
That so we may
At least be in Love's way;
And in these chaste wars, while the wing'd wounds flee
So fast 'twixt Him and thee,

My breast may catch the kiss of some kind dart,
Though as at second hand, from either heart.

VIII.

    O you, your own best darts,
    Dear, doleful hearts!
    Hail! and strike home, and make me see
That wounded bosoms their own weapons be.
    Come wounds! come darts!
    Nail'd hands! and piercèd hearts!
Come your whole selves, Sorrow's great Son and
    mother!
    Nor grudge a younger brother
Of griefs his portion, who (had all their due)
One single wound should not have left for you.

IX.

    Shall I set there
    So deep a share,
    (Dear wounds!), and only now
In sorrows draw no dividend with you?
    O be more wise,
    If not more soft, mine eyes!
Flow, tardy founts! and into decent showers
    Dissolve my days and hours.
And if thou yet (faint soul!) defer
To bleed with Him, fail not to weep with her.

X.

    Rich queen, lend some relief;
    At least an alms of grief,
    To a heart who by sad right of sin
Could prove the whole sum (too sure) due to him.
    By all those stings
    Of Love, sweet-bitter things,
Which these torn hands transcribed on thy true heart;
    O teach mine, too, the art
To study Him so, till we mix
Wounds, and become one crucifix.

XI.

    Oh, let me suck the wine
    So long of this chaste Vine,
    Till drunk of the dear wounds, I be
A lost thing to the world, as it to me.
    O faithful friend
    Of me and of my end!
Fold up my life in love; and lay't beneath
    My dear Lord's vital death.
Lo, heart, thy hope's whole plea! her precious breath
Pour'd out in prayers for thee; thy Lord's in death

Upon the Bleeding Crucifix:

A Song.

I.

Jesu, no more! It is full tide;
   From Thy hands and from Thy feet,
From Thy head, and from Thy side,
   All the purple rivers meet.

II.

What need Thy fair head bear a part
   In showers, as if Thine eyes had none?
What need they help to drown Thy heart,
   That strives in torrents of its own?

III.

Water'd by the showers they bring,
   The thorns that Thy blest brow encloses
(A cruel and a costly spring)
   Conceive proud hopes of proving roses.*

IV.

Thy restless feet now cannot go
   For us and our eternal good,
As they were ever wont. What though?
   They swim, alas! in their own flood.

---

* This Stanza is not given in the 1652 Edition: it occurs in ed. of 1646.—Ed.

V.

Thy hand to give Thou canst not lift;
   Yet wilt Thy hand still giving be.
It gives, but O itself's the gift:
   It gives though bound; though bound 'tis free.

VI.

But, O Thy side! Thy deep-digg'd side!
   That hath a double Nilus going:
Nor ever was the Pharian tide
   Half so fruitful, half so flowing.

VII.

No hair so small, but pays his river
   To this Red Sea of Thy blood;
Their little channels can deliver
   Something to the general flood.

VIII.

But while I speak, whither are run
   All the rivers named before?
I counted wrong: there is but one;
   But O that one is one all o'er.

IX.

Rain-swol'n rivers may rise proud,
   Bent all to drown and overflow;
But when indeed all's overflow'd,
   They themselves are drownèd too.

X.

This Thy blood's deluge (a dire chance,
　Dear Lord, to Thee) to us is found
A deluge of deliverance ;
　A deluge lest we should be drown'd,
　　Ne'er wast Thou in a sense so sadly true,
　　The well of living waters, Lord, till now.

—:o:—

Upon The Crown of Thorns taken down from the Head of Our Blessed Lord, all Bloody.

Know'st thou this, Soldier? 'tis a much changed plant, which yet
　　　　　　　　　　Thyself didst set,
'Tis changed indeed; did Autumn e'er such beauties bring
　　　　　　　　　　To shame his Spring?*
Oh! who so hard a husbandman could ever find
　　　　　　　　　　A soil so kind?
Is not the soil a kind one (think ye) that returns
　　　　　　　　　　Roses for thorns?

　* Lines third and fourth are not given in the ed. of 1652.—Ed.

Upon The Body of Our Blessed Lord, Naked and Bloody.

They have left Thee naked, Lord ; O that they had !
    This garment too I would they had denied.
Thee with Thyself they have too richly clad ;
    Opening the purple wardrobe in Thy side.
O never could there be garment too good
For Thee to wear, but this of Thine own blood.

—:o:—

The Hymn of St. Thomas,

IN ADORATION OF THE BLESSED SACRAMENT.

With all the powers my poor heart hath
Of humble love and loyal faith,
Thus low (my hidden life !) I bow to Thee,
Whom too much love hath bow'd more low for me.
Down, down, proud Sense! discourses die!
Keep close, my soul's inquiring eye!
Nor touch nor taste must look for more,
But each sit still in his own door.

    Your ports are all superfluous here,
Save that which lets in Faith, the ear.
Faith is my skill ; Faith can believe
As fast as Love new laws can give.

Faith is my force : Faith strength affords
To keep pace with those pow'rful words.
And words more sure, more sweet than they,
Love could not think, Truth could not say.

O let Thy wretch find that relief
Thou didst afford the faithful thief.
Plead for me, Love! allege and show
That Faith has farther here to go,
And less to lean on : because then
Though hid as God, wounds writ Thee man ;
Thomas might touch, none but might see
At least the suffering side of Thee ;
And that too was Thyself which Thee did cover,
But here ev'n that's hid too which hides the other.

Sweet, consider then, that I,
Though allowed nor hand nor eye
To reach at Thy loved face ; nor can
Taste Thee God, or touch Thee man,
Both yet believe, and witness Thee
My Lord too, and my God, as loud as he.

Help, Lord, my faith, my hope increase,
And fill my portion in Thy peace :
Give love for life ; nor let my days
Grow, but in new powers to Thy name and praise.

O dear memorial of that Death
Which lives still, and allows us breath !

Rich, royal food! Bountiful bread!
Whose use denies us to the dead;
Whose vital gust alone can give
The same leave both to eat and live.
Live ever, bread of loves, and be
My life, my soul, my surer self to me.

O soft, self-wounding Pelican!
Whose breast weeps balm for wounded man:
Ah, this way bend Thy benign flood
To a bleeding heart that gasps for blood.
That blood, whose least drops sovereign be
To wash my worlds of sins from me.

Come Love! come Lord! and that long day
For which I languish, come away.
When this dry soul those eyes shall see,
And drink the unseal'd source of Thee:
When Glory's sun, Faith's shades shall chase,
And for Thy veil give me Thy face. *Amen.*

Lauda Sion Salvatorem:

THE HYMN FOR THE BLESSED SACRAMENT.

I.

Rise, royal Sion! rise and sing
Thy soul's kind Shepherd, thy heart's King.
Stretch all thy powers; call if you can
Harps of heaven to hands of man.
This sovereign subject sits above
The best ambition of thy love.

II.

Lo, the Bread of Life, this day's
Triumphant text, provokes thy praise;
The living and life-giving bread,
To the great twelve distributed;
When Life, Himself, at point to die
Of love, was His Own legacy.

III.

Come, Love! and let us work a song
Loud and pleasant, sweet and long;
Let lips and hearts lift high the noise
Of so just and solemn joys,
Which on His white brows this bright day
Shall hence for ever bear away.

IV.

Lo, the new law of a new Lord,
With a new Lamb blesses the board :
The agèd Pascha pleads not years,
But spies Love's dawn, and disappears.
Types yield to truths ; shades shrink away ;
And their Night dies into our Day.

V.

But lest that die too, we are bid
Ever to do what He once did :
And by a mindful, mystic breath,
That we may live, revive His death :
With a well-bless'd bread and wine,
Transumed, and taught to turn divine.

VI.

The Heaven-instructed house of Faith
Here a holy dictate hath,
That they but lend their form and face :—
Themselves with reverence leave their place,
Nature, and name, to be made good,
By a nobler bread, more needful blood.

VII.

Where Nature's laws no leave will give,
Bold Faith takes heart, and dares believe
In different species : name not things,
Himself to me my Saviour brings ;

As meat in that, as drink in this,
But still in both one Christ He is.

VIII.

The receiving mouth here makes
Nor wound nor breach in what he takes.
Let one, or one thousand be
Here dividers, single he
Bears home no less, all they no more,
Nor leave they both less than before.

IX.

Though in itself this sov'reign Feast
Be all the same to every guest,
Yet on the same (life-meaning) Bread
The child of death eats himself dead :
Nor is 't Love's fault, but Sin's dire skill
That thus from Life can death distil.

X.

When the blest signs thou broke shalt see,
Hold but thy faith entire as He,
Who, howsoe'er clad, cannot come
Less than whole Christ in every crumb.
In broken forms a stable Faith
Untouch'd her precious total hath.

XI.

Lo, the life-food of angels then
Bow'd to the lowly mouths of men!

The children's Bread, the Bridegroom's Wine,
Not to be cast to dogs or swine.

XII.

Lo, the full, final Sacrifice
On which all figures fix'd their eyes:
The ransom'd Isaac, and his ram;
The manna, and the paschal lamb.

XIII.

Jesu Master, just and true!
Our food, and faithful Shepherd too!
O by Thyself vouchsafe to keep,
As with Thyself Thou feed'st Thy sheep.

XIV.

O let that love which thus makes Thee
Mix with our low mortality,
Lift our lean souls, and set us up
Convictors of Thine Own full cup,
Coheirs of saints.   That so all may
Drink the same wine; and the same way:
Nor change the pasture, but the place,
To feed of Thee in Thine Own face.   *Amen.*

Dies Iræ, Dies Illa:

THE HYMN OF THE CHURCH, IN MEDITATION OF THE DAY OF JUDGMENT.

I.

Hear'st thou, my soul, what serious things
Both the Psalm and Sybil sings
Of a sure Judge, from Whose sharp ray
The World in flames shall fly away.

II.

O that fire! before whose face
Heaven and Earth shall find no place.
O those eyes! Whose angry light
Must be the day of that dread night.

III.

O that trump! whose blast shall run
An even round with the circling sun,
And urge the murmuring graves to bring
Pale mankind forth to meet his King.

IV.

Horror of Nature, Hell, and Death!
When a deep groan from beneath
Shall cry, 'We come, we come,' and all
The caves of Night answer one call.

V.

O that Book! whose leaves so bright
Will set the World in severe light.
O that Judge! Whose hand, Whose eye
None can endure; yet none can fly.

VI.

Ah then, poor soul, what wilt thou say?
And to what patron choose to pray?
When stars themselves shall stagger, and
The most firm foot no more then stand.

VII.

But Thou givest leave (dread Lord!) that we
Take shelter from Thyself in Thee;
And with the wings of Thine Own dove
Fly to Thy sceptre of soft love.

VIII.

Dear, remember in that Day
Who was the cause Thou cam'st this way.
Thy sheep was stray'd; and Thou would'st be
Even lost Thyself in seeking me.

IX.

Shall all that labour, all that cost
Of love, and even that loss, be lost?
And this loved soul, judged worth no less
Than all that way and weariness?

X.

Just mercy, then, Thy reck'ning be
With my Price, and not with me ;
'Twas paid at first with too much pain,
To be paid twice ; or once, in vain.

XI.

Mercy (my Judge), mercy I cry
With blushing cheek and bleeding eye :
The conscious colours of my sin
Are red without and pale within.

XII.

O let Thine Own soft bowels pay
Thyself, and so discharge that day.
If Sin can sigh, Love can forgive :
O say the word, my soul shall live !

XIII.

Those mercies which Thy Mary found,
Or who Thy cross confess'd and crown'd,
Hope tells my heart, the same loves be
Still alive, and still for me.

XIV.

Though both my prayers and tears combine,
Both worthless are ; for they are mine.
But Thou Thy bounteous Self still be ;
And show Thou art, by saving me.

XV.

O when Thy last frown shall proclaim
The flocks of goats to folds of flame,
And all Thy lost sheep found shall be;
Let, 'Come, ye blessed,' then call me.

XVI.

When the dread '*Ite*' shall divide
Those limbs of death from Thy left side;
Let those life-speaking lips command
That I inherit Thy right hand.

XVII.

O hear a suppliant heart, all crusht
And crumbled into contrite dust.
My hope, my fear, my Judge, my Friend!
Take charge of me, and of my end.

—:o:—

S. Maria Major.

Dilectus meus mihi, et ego illi, qui pascitur inter lilia.—*Cant.* ii.

THE HYMN, O GLORIOSA DOMINA.

Hail, most high, most humble one!
Above the world, below thy Son;
Whose blush the moon beauteously mars,
And stains the timorous light of stars.
He that made all things had not done

Till He had made Himself thy Son.
The whole World's host would be thy guest,
And board Himself at thy rich breast.
O boundless hospitality!
The Feast of all things feeds on thee.
 The first Eve, mother of our Fall,
Ere she bore any one, slew all.
Of her unkind gift might we have
Th' inheritance of a hasty grave:
Quick buried in the wanton tomb
  Of one forbidden bit,
Had not a better fruit forbidden it.
  Had not thy healthful womb
The World's new eastern window been,
And given us heaven again in giving Him.
Thine was the rosy dawn that sprung the day,
Which renders all the stars she stole away.
 Let then the agèd World be wise, and all
Prove nobly here unnatural:
'Tis gratitude to forget that other,
And call the maiden Eve their mother.
 Ye redeem'd nations far and near,
Applaud your happy selves in her;
(All you to whom this love belongs)
And keep 't alive with lasting songs.
 Let hearts and lips speak loud and say,
Hail, door of life, and source of Day!
The door was shut, the fountain seal'd,

Yet Light was seen and Life reveal'd.
The door was shut, yet let in day,
The fountain seal'd, yet life found way.
   Glory to Thee, great virgin's Son!
In bosom of Thy Father's bliss.
   The same to Thee, sweet Spirit! be done:
As ever shall be, was, and is. *Amen.*

— :o: —

On The Glorious Assumption of our Blessed Lady.

THE HYMN.

Hark! she is call'd, the parting hour is come;
Take thy farewell, poor World, Heaven must go home.
A piece of heavenly earth, purer and brighter
Than the chaste stars whose choice lamps come to light her,
Whilst through the crystal orbs clearer than they
She climbs, and makes a far more Milky Way.
She's call'd! Hark, how the dear immortal Dove
Sighs to His silver mate: 'Rise up, my love!'
Rise up, my fair, my spotless one!
The Winter's past, the rain is gone:
The Spring is come, the flowers appear,
No sweets (save thou) are wanting here.
    Come away, my love!
    Come away, my dove!
      Cast off delay;

THE ASSUMPTION OF THE VIRGIN.

      The court of Heaven is come
      To wait upon thee home;
        Come, come away.
The flowers appear,
Or quickly would, wert thou once here.
The Spring is come, or if it stay
'Tis to keep time with thy delay.
The rain is gone, except so much as we
Detain in needful tears to weep the want of thee.
      The Winter's past,
      Or if he make less haste
His answer is why she does so,
If Summer come not, how can Winter go?
      Come away, come away!
The shrill winds chide, the waters weep thy stay;
The fountains murmur, and each loftiest tree
Bows lowest his leafy top, to look for thee.
      Come away, my love!
      Come away, my dove! etc.

She's call'd again.   And will she go?
When Heaven bids come, who can say no?
Heaven calls her, and she must away,
Heaven will not, and she cannot stay.
Go then; go, glorious on the golden wings
Of the bright youth of Heaven, that sings
Under so sweet a burthen.   Go,
Since thy dread Son will have it so:

And while thou go'st, our song and we
Will, as we may, reach after thee.
Hail, holy queen of humble hearts!
We in thy praise will have our parts.
And though thy dearest looks must now give light
To none but the blest heavens, whose bright
Beholders, lost in sweet delight,
Feed for ever their fair sight
With those divinest eyes, which we
And our dark world no more shall see;
Though our poor eyes are parted so,
Yet shall our lips never let go
Thy gracious name, but to the last,
Our loving song shall hold it fast.*

  Thy precious name shall be
  Thyself to us; and we
   With holy care will keep it by us,
    We to the last
    Will hold it fast,
   And no Assumption shall deny us.
  All the sweetest showers
  Of our fairest flowers
  Will we strow upon it.
  Though our sweets cannot make
  It sweeter, they can take
  Themselves new sweetness from it.

* The edition of 1652 lacks this and the preceding nine lines. They occur in the 1648 version.—Ed.

Maria, men and angels sing,
Maria, mother of our King.
Live, rosy princess, live! and may the bright
Crown of a most incomparable light
Embrace thy radiant brows. O may the best
Of everlasting joys bathe thy white breast.
Live, our chaste love, the holy mirth
Of Heaven; the humble pride of Earth.
Live, crown of women; queen of men:
Live, mistress of our song. And when
Our weak desires have done their best,
Sweet angels come, and sing the rest.

—:o:—

Saint Mary Magdalene, or The Weeper.

Lo! where a wounded heart with bleeding eyes conspire,
Is she a flaming fountain, or a weeping fire?

THE WEEPER.

I.*

Hail, sister springs!
Parents of silver-footed rills!
Ever-bubbling things!
Thawing crystal! snowy hills
Still spending, never spent! I mean
Thy fair eyes, sweet Magdalene!

* In the main, the succession of stanzas as in 1646 edition has been adopted.—Ed.

II.

Heavens thy fair eyes be;
Heavens of ever-falling stars.
'Tis seed-time still with thee;
And stars thou sow'st, whose harvest dares
Promise the Earth to countershine
Whatever makes heaven's forehead fine.

III.

But we are deceived all:
Stars indeed they are too true:
For they but seem to fall,
As Heaven's other spangles do:
It is not for our Earth and us,
To shine in things so precious.

IV.

Upwards thou dost weep,
Heaven's bosom drinks the gentle stream.
Where th' milky rivers creep,
Thine floats above, and is the cream.
Waters above th' heavens, what they be
We are taught best by thy tears and thee.

V.

Every morn from hence,
A brisk cherub something sips,
Whose sacred influence
Adds sweetness to his sweetest lips;

SAINT MARY MAGDALENE.

Then to his music ; and his song
Tastes of this breakfast all day long.*

VI.

When some new bright guest
Takes up among the stars a room,
And Heaven will make a feast :
Angels with crystal phials come
And draw from these full eyes of thine,
Their Master's water, their own wine.

VII.

The dew no more will weep
The primrose's pale cheek to deck :
The dew no more will sleep
Nuzzel'd in the lily's neck ;
Much rather would it be thy tear,
And leave them both to tremble here.

VIII.

Not the soft gold which
Steals from the amber-weeping tree,
Makes Sorrow half so rich
As the drops distill'd from thee.
Sorrow's best jewels lie in these
Caskets, of which Heaven keeps the keys.

---

* We drop here a stanza of our 1652 text, for the reason that it was inadvertantly inserted there, belonging, without question, to another poem.—Ed.

IX.

When Sorrow would be seen
In her brightest majesty:
(For she is a Queen):
Then is she dress'd by none but thee.
Then, and only then, she wears
Her proudest pearls: I mean, thy tears.

X.

Not in the Evening eyes,
When they red with weeping are
For the Sun that dies;
Sits Sorrow with a face so fair.
Nowhere but here did ever meet
Sweetness so sad, sadness so sweet.

XI.

Sadness all the while
She sits in such a throne as this,
Can do nought but smile,
Nor believes she Sadness is:
Gladness itself would be more glad,
To be made so sweetly sad.*

XII.

There's no need at all,
That the balsam-sweating bough
So coyly should let fall
His med'cinable tears; for now

---

* This stanza is restored from the version of 1646.—Ed.

Nature has learn'd to extract a dew
More sovereign and sweet, from you.

XIII.

Yet let the poor drops weep,
(Weeping is the ease of Woe) :
Softly let them creep,
Sad that they are vanquish'd so.
They, though to others no relief,
Balsam may be for their own grief.

XIV.

Golden though he be,
Golden Tagus murmurs though.
Were his way by thee,
Content and quiet he would go ;
So much more rich would he esteem
Thy silver, than his golden stream.

XV.

Well does the May that lies
Smiling in thy cheeks, confess
The April in thine eyes ;
Mutual sweetness they express.
No April e'er lent kinder showers,
Nor May returned more faithful flowers.

XVI.

O cheeks ! Beds of chaste loves,
By your own showers seasonably dashed.
Eyes ! Nests of milky doves,
In your own wells decently washed.

O wit of Love! that thus could place
Fountain and garden in one face.

XVII.

 O sweet contest! of woes
 With loves; of tears with smiles disputing!
 O fair and friendly foes,
 Each other kissing and confuting!
While rain and sunshine, cheeks and eyes,
Close in kind contrarieties.

XVIII.

 But can these fair floods be
 Friends with the bosom-fires that fill thee?
 Can so great flames agree
 Eternal tears should thus distil thee?
O floods! O fires! O suns! O showers!
Mixed and made friends by Love's sweet powers.

XIX.

 'Twas his well-pointed dart
 That digged these wells, and dressed this wine;
 And taught the wounded heart
 The way into these weeping eyne.
Vain loves avaunt! bold hands forbear!
The Lamb hath dipped His white foot here.

XX.

 And now where'er He stays,
 Among the Galilean mountains,

Or more unwelcome ways;
He's followed by two faithful fountains;
Two walking baths, two weeping motions,
Portable, and compendious oceans.

XXI.

O thou, thy Lord's fair store!
In thy so rich and rare expenses,
Even when He showed most poor
He might provoke the wealth of princes.
What Prince's wanton'st pride e'er could
Wash with silver, wipe with gold?

XXII.

Who is that King, but He
Who calls't His crown, to be called thine,
That thus can boast to be
Waited on by a wandering mine,
A voluntary mint, that strews
Warm, silver showers where'er He goes?

XXIII.

O precious prodigal!
Fair spend-thrift of thyself! thy measure
(Merciless love!) is all.
Even to the last pearl in thy treasure:
All places, times, and objects be
Thy tears' sweet opportunity.

XXIV.

Does the Night arise?
Still thy tears do fall and fall.
Does Night loose her eyes?
Still the fountain weeps for all.
Let Night or Day do what they will,
Thou hast thy task: thou weepest still.

XXV.

Does thy song lull the air?
Thy falling tears keep faithful time.
Does thy sweet-breathed prayer
Up in clouds of incense climb?
Still at each sigh, that is, each stop,
A bead, that is, a tear, does drop.

XXVI.

At these thy weeping gates
(Watching their watery motion),
Each wingèd moment waits:
Takes his tear, and gets him gone.
By thine eyes' tinct ennobled thus,
Time lays him up; he's precious.

XXVII.

Time, as by thee He passes,
Makes thy ever-watery eyes
His hour-glasses.
By them His steps He rectifies.

The sands He used no longer please,
For His own sands He'll use thy seas.

XXVIII.

Not, 'so long she livèd,'
Shall thy tomb report of thee ;
But, 'so long she grievèd' :
Thus must we date thy memory.
Others by moments, months, and years
Measure their ages ; thou, by tears.

XXIX.

So do perfumes expire,
So sigh tormented sweets, opprest
With proud unpitying fire,
Such tears the suffering rose, that's vext
With ungentle flames, does shed,
Sweating in a too warm bed.

XXX.

Say, ye bright brothers,
The fugitive sons of those fair eyes,
Your fruitful mothers !
What make you here ? what hopes can 'tice
You to be born ? what cause can borrow
You from those nests of noble sorrow ?

XXXI.

Whither away so fast ?
For sure the sluttish earth

Your sweetness cannot taste,
  Nor does the dust deserve your birth.
Sweet, whither hast you then? O say
Why you trip so fast away?

XXXII.

  We go not to seek
The darlings of Aurora's bed,
  The rose's modest cheek,
Nor the violet's humble head.
Though the field's eyes too Weepers be,
Because they want such tears as we.

XXXIII.

  Much less mean we to trace
The fortune of inferior gems,
  Preferr'd to some proud face,
Or perched upon fear'd diadems:
Crown'd heads are toys. We go to meet
A worthy object, our Lord's feet.

A Hymn to the Name and Honour of The Admirable Saint Teresa:

Foundress of the Reformation of the Discalced Carmelites, both men and women; a woman for angelical height of speculation, for masculine courage of performance, more than a woman, who yet a child outran maturity, and durst plot a martyrdom.

Love, thou art absolute sole lord
Of life and death. To prove the word
We'll now appeal to none of all
Those thy old soldiers, great and tall,
Ripe men of martyrdom, that could reach down,
With strong arms, their triumphant crown ;
Such as could with lusty breath,
Speak loud into the face of Death
Their great Lord's glorious name, to none
Of those whose spacious bosoms spread a throne
For Love at large to fill; spare blood and sweat :
And see him take a private seat,
Making his mansion in the mild
And milky soul of a soft child.
   Scarce has she learnt to lisp the name
Of martyr; yet she thinks it shame
Life should so long play with that breath
Which spent can buy so brave a death.
She never undertook to know
What Death with Love should have to do ;

Nor has she e'er yet understood
Why to show love, she should shed blood,
Yet though she cannot tell you why,
She can love, and she can die.

Scarce has she blood enough to make
A guilty sword blush for her sake;
Yet has she a heart dares hope to prove
How much less strong is Death than Love.

Be Love but there; let poor six years
Be posed with the maturest fears
Man trembles at, you straight shall find
Love knows no nonage, nor the mind;
'Tis love, not years or limbs that can
Make the martyr, or the man.
Love touched her heart, and lo it beats
High, and burns with such brave heats;
Such thirsts to die, as dares drink up
A thousand cold deaths in one cup.
Good reason; for she breathes all fire;
Her white breast heaves with strong desire
Of what she may, with fruitless wishes,
Seek for amongst her mother's kisses.

Since 'tis not to be had at home
She'll travel to a martyrdom.
No home for hers confesses she
But where she may a martyr be.

She'll to the Moors; and trade with them
For this unvalued diadem:

She'll offer them her dearest breath,
With Christ's name in't, in change for death:
She'll bargain with them ; and will give
Them God ; teach them how to live
In Him : or, if they this deny,
For Him she'll teach them how to die :
So shall she leave amongst them sown
Her Lord's blood : or at least her own.

   Farewell then, all the World! adieu!
Teresa is no more for you.
Farewell, all pleasures, sports, and joys
(Never till now esteemèd toys)
Farewell, whatever dear may be,
Mother's arms, or father's knee :
Farewell house, and farewell home!
She's for the Moors, and martyrdom.

   Sweet, not so fast ! lo, thy fair Spouse,
Whom thou seek'st with so swift vows ;
Calls thee back, and bids thee come
T' embrace a milder martyrdom.

   Blest powers forbid, thy tender life
Should bleed upon a barbarous knife :
Or some base hand have power to rase
Thy breast's chaste cabinet, and uncase
A soul kept there so sweet : O no,
Wise Heaven will never have it so.
Thou art Love's victim ; and must die
A death more mystical and high :

Into Love's arms thou shalt let fall
A still-surviving funeral.
His is the dart must make the death
Whose stroke shall taste thy hallowed breath;
A dart thrice dipp'd in that rich flame
Which writes thy Spouse's radiant name
Upon the roof of Heaven, where aye
It shines; and with a sovereign ray
Beats bright upon the burning faces
Of souls which in that Name's sweet graces
Find everlasting smiles: so rare,
So spiritual, pure, and fair
Must be th' immortal instrument
Upon whose choice point shall be sent
A life so loved: and that there be
Fit executioners for thee,
The fairest and first-born sons of fire,
Blest seraphim, shall leave their quire,
And turn Love's soldiers, upon thee
To exercise their archery.

  O how oft shalt thou complain
Of a sweet and subtle pain:
Of intolerable joys:
Of a death, in which who dies
Loves his death, and dies again,
And would for ever so be slain.
And lives, and dies; and knows not why
To live, but that he thus may never leave to die.

How kindly will thy gentle heart
Kiss the sweetly-killing dart!
And close in his embraces keep
Those delicious wounds, that weep
Balsam to heal themselves with: thus
When these thy deaths, so numerous,
Shall all at last die into one,
And melt thy soul's sweet mansion;
Like a soft lump of incense, hasted
By too hot a fire, and wasted
Into perfuming clouds, so fast
Shalt thou exhale to Heaven at last
In a resolving sigh, and then
O what? Ask not the tongues of men;
Angels cannot tell; suffice
Thyself shall feel thine own full joys,
And hold them fast for ever there.
So soon as thou shalt first appear,
The moon of maiden stars, thy white
Mistress, attended by such bright
Souls as thy shining self, shall come,
And in her first ranks make thee room;
Where 'mongst her snowy family
Immortal welcomes wait for thee.

O what delight, when revealed Life shall stand,
And teach thy lips Heaven with His hand;
On which thou now may'st to thy wishes
Heap up thy consecrated kisses.

What joys shall seize thy soul, when she,
Bending her blessed eyes on Thee,
(Those second smiles of Heaven,) shall dart
Her mild rays through Thy melting heart.

 Angels, thy old friends, there shall greet thee,
Glad at their own home now to meet thee.

 All thy good works which went before
And waited for thee, at the door,
Shall own thee there; and all in one
Weave a constellation
Of crowns, with which the King thy Spouse
Shall build up thy triumphant brows.

 All thy old woes shall now smile on thee,
And thy pains sit bright upon thee,
All thy sorrows here shall shine,
All thy sufferings be divine:
Tears shall take comfort, and turn gems,
And wrongs repent to diadems.
Even thy death shall live; and new-
Dress the soul, that erst he slew.
Thy wounds shall blush to such bright scars
As keep account of the Lamb's wars.

 Those rare works where thou shalt leave writ
Love's noble history, with wit
Taught thee by none but Him, while here
They feed our souls, shall clothe thine there.
Each heavenly word, by whose hid flame
Our hard hearts shall strike fire, the same

Shall flourish on thy brows, and be
Both fire to us and flame to thee;
Whose light shall live bright in thy face
By glory, in our hearts by grace.

  Thou shalt look round about, and see
Thousands of crown'd souls throng to be
Themselves thy crown: sons of thy vows,
The virgin-births with which thy sovereign Spouse
Made fruitful thy fair soul. Go now
And with them all about thee, bow
To Him; put on, (He'll say,) put on
(My rosy love) that thy rich zone
Sparkling with the sacred flames
Of thousand souls, whose happy names
Heaven keep upon thy score: (Thy bright
Life brought them first to kiss the light,
That kindled them to stars,) and so
Thou with the Lamb, thy Lord, shalt go,
And wheresoe'er He sets His white
Steps, walk with Him those ways of light,
Which who in death would live to see,
Must learn in life to die like thee.

An Apology For The Fore-Going Hymn,

AS HAVING BEEN WRIT WHEN THE AUTHOR WAS YET AMONG THE PROTESTANTS.

Thus have I back again to thy bright name,
(Fair flood of holy fires!) transfus'd the flame
I took from reading thee; 'tis to thy wrong,
I know, that in my weak and worthless song
Thou here art set to shine, where thy full day
Scarce dawns. O pardon, if I dare to say
Thine own dear books are guilty. For from thence
I learn'd to know that Love is eloquence.
That hopeful maxim gave me heart to try
If, what to other tongues is tuned so high,
Thy praise might not speak English too: forbid
(By all thy mysteries that there lie hid)
Forbid it, mighty Love! let no fond hate
Of names and words so far prejudicate.
Souls are not Spaniards too: one friendly flood
Of baptism blends them all into a blood.
Christ's faith makes but one body of all souls,
And Love's that body's soul; no law controls
Our free traffic for Heaven; we may maintain
Peace, sure, with piety, though it come from Spain.
What soul soe'er in any language, can
Speak Heav'n like her's, is my soul's countryman.
O 'tis not Spanish, but 'tis Heav'n she speaks!
'Tis Heav'n that lies in ambush there, and breaks

From thence into the wondering reader's breast;
Who feels his warm heart hatch into a nest
Of little eagles and young loves, whose high
Flights scorn the lazy dust, and things that die.
There are enow whose draughts (as deep as Hell)
Drink up all Spain in sack. Let my soul swell
With the strong wine of Love : let others swim
In puddles; we will pledge this seraphim
Bowls full of richer blood than blush of grape
Was ever guilty of. Change we our shape,
(My soul) some drink from men to beasts, O then
Drink we till we prove more, not less than men,
And turn not beasts, but angels. Let the King
Me ever into these His cellars bring,
Where flows such wine as we can have of none
But Him Who trod the wine-press all alone :
Wine of youth, life, and the sweet deaths of Love ;
Wine of immortal mixture ; which can prove
Its tincture from the rosy nectar ; wine
That can exalt weak earth ; and so refine
Our dust, that, at one draught, Mortality
May drink itself up, and forget to die.

The Flaming Heart:

Upon the book and picture of the seraphical Saint Teresa, as she is usually expressed with a seraphim beside her.

Well-meaning readers! you that come as friends,
And catch the precious name this piece pretends;
Make not too much haste to admire
That fair-cheek'd fallacy of fire.
That is a seraphim, they say,
And this the great Teresia.
Readers, be ruled by me; and make
Here a well-placed and wise mistake;
You must transpose the picture quite,
And spell it wrong to read it right:
Read him for her, and her for him,
And call the saint the seraphim.
   Painter, what didst thou understand
To put her dart into his hand?
See, even the years and size of him
Shows this the mother-seraphim.
This is the mistress-flame; and duteous he
Her happy fire-works, here, comes down to see.
O most poor-spirited of men!
Had thy cold pencil kiss'd her pen,
Thou couldst not so unkindly err
To show us this faint shade for her.
Why, man, this speaks pure mortal frame;

And mocks with female frost Love's manly flame.
One would suspect thou meant'st to paint
Some weak, inferior, woman-saint.
But had thy pale-faced purple took
Fire from the burning cheeks of that bright book,
Thou wouldst on her have heap'd up all
That could be found seraphical;
Whate'er this youth of fire wears fair,
Rosy fingers, radiant hair,
Glowing cheek, and glist'ring wings,
All those fair and fragrant things,
But before all, that fiery dart
Had fill'd the hand of this great heart.

 Do then, as equal right requires;
Since his the blushes be, and her's the fires,
Resume and rectify thy rude design;
Undress thy seraphim into mine;
Redeem this injury of thy art,
Give him the veil, give her the dart.
Give him the veil, that he may cover
The red cheeks of a rivall'd lover;
Ashamed that our world now can show
Nests of new seraphims here below.

 Give her the dart, for it is she
(Fair youth) shoots both thy shaft and thee;
Say, all ye wise and well-pierced hearts
That live and die amidst her darts,
What is't your tasteful spirits do prove

In that rare life of her, and Love?
Say, and bear witness. Sends she not
A seraphim at every shot?
What magazines of immortal arms there shine!
Heaven's great artillery in each love-spun line.
Give then the dart to her who gives the flame;
Give him the veil, who gives the shame.

But if it be the frequent fate
Of worst faults to be fortunate;
If all's prescription; and proud wrong
Hearkens not to an humble song;
For all the gallantry of him,
Give me the suffering seraphim.
His be the bravery of all those bright things,
The glowing cheeks, the glistering wings;
The rosy hand, the radiant dart;
Leave her alone the flaming heart.

Leave her that; and thou shalt leave her
Not one loose shaft, but Love's whole quiver;
For in Love's field was never found
A nobler weapon than a wound.
Love's passives are his activ'st part:
The wounded is the wounding heart.
O heart! the equal poise of Love's both parts,
Big alike with wound and darts.
Live in these conquering leaves; live all the same;
And walk through all tongues one triumphant flame.
Live here, great heart; and love, and die, and kill;

And bleed, and wound; and yield and conquer still.
Let this immortal life where'er it comes
Walk in a crowd of loves and martyrdoms.
Let mystic deaths wait on't; and wise souls be
The love-slain witnesses of this life of thee.
  O sweet incendiary! show here thy art,
Upon this carcass of a hard cold heart;
Let all thy scatter'd shafts of light that play
Among the leaves of thy large books of day,
Combined against this breast at once break in
And take away from me myself and sin;
This gracious robbery shall thy bounty be,
And my best fortunes such fair spoils of me.
O thou undaunted daughter of desires!
By all thy dower of lights and fires;
By all the eagle in thee, all the dove;
By all thy lives and deaths of love;
By thy large draughts of intellectual day,
And by thy thirsts of love more large than they;
By all thy brim-fill'd bowls of fierce desire,
By thy last morning's draught of liquid fire;
By the full kingdom of that final kiss
'That seized thy parting soul, and seal'd thee His;
By all the Heaven thou hast in Him
(Fair sister of the seraphim!)
By all of Him we have in thee;
Leave nothing of myself in me.
Let me so read thy life, that I
Unto all life of mine may die.

A Song.

Lord, when the sense of Thy sweet grace
Sends up my soul to seek Thy face,
Thy blessed eyes breed such desire,
I die in Love's delicious fire.

O Love, I am thy sacrifice!
Be still triumphant, blessed eyes!
Still shine on me, fair suns! that I
Still may behold, though still I die.

SECOND PART.

Though still I die, I live again;
Still longing so to be still slain;
So gainful is such loss of breath;
I die even in desire of death.

Still live in me this longing strife
Of living death and dying life;
For while Thou sweetly slayest me
Dead to myself, I live in Thee.

Prayer:

AN ODE WHICH WAS PREFIXED TO A LITTLE PRAYER-BOOK GIVEN TO A YOUNG GENTLEWOMAN.

Lo here a little volume, but great book !
    (Fear it not, sweet,
    It is no hypocrite),
Much larger in itself than in its look.
    A nest of new-born sweets ;
    Whose native fires disdaining
    To lie thus folded, and complaining
    Of these ignoble sheets,
    Affect more comely bands
    (Fair one) from thy kind hands ;
    And confidently look
    To find the rest
Of a rich binding in your breast.
It is, in one choice handful, Heaven ; and all
Heaven's royal host ; encamp'd thus small
To prove that true, Schools use to tell,
Ten thousand angels in one point can dwell.
It is Love's great artillery
Which here contracts itself, and comes to lie
Close-couch'd in your white bosom ; and from thence,
As from a snowy fortress of defence,
Against the ghostly foes to take your part,
And fortify the hold of your chaste heart.
It is an armoury of light ;

Let constant use but keep it bright,
    You'll find it yields,
To holy hands and humble hearts,
    More swords and shields
Than sin hath snares, or Hell hath darts.
    Only be sure
    The hands be pure
That hold these weapons; and the eyes
    Those of turtles, chaste and true;
Wakeful and wise:
    Here is a friend shall fight for you,
Hold but this book before your heart,
Let prayer alone to play his part;
But O the heart,
That studies this high art,
Must be a sure house-keeper:
And yet no sleeper.
Dear soul, be strong!
Mercy will come ere long,
And bring his bosom fraught with blessings,
Flowers of never-fading graces,
To make immortal dressings
For worthy souls, whose wise embraces
Store up themselves for Him, Who is alone
The Spouse of virgins, and the virgin's Son.
But if the noble Bridegroom, when He come,
    Shall find the loitering heart from home;
    Leaving her chaste abode

PRAYER.

    To gad abroad
Among the gay mates of the god of flies ;
    To take her pleasure, and to play
    And keep the devil's holyday ;
To dance in th' sunshine of some smiling
    But beguiling
Sphere of sweet and sugar'd lies ;
    Some slippery pair,
    Of false, perhaps as fair,
Flattering but forswearing, eyes ;
Doubtless some other heart
    Will get the start
Meanwhile, and stepping in before,
Will take possession of the sacred store
Of hidden sweets and holy joys ;
Words which are not heard with ears
('Those tumultuous shops of noise)
Effectual whispers, whose still voice
The soul itself more feels than hears ;
Amorous languishments, luminous trances ;
Sights which are not seen with eyes ;
Spiritual and soul-piercing glances,
Whose pure and subtle lightning flies
Home to the heart, and sets the house on fire
And melts it down in sweet desire :
    Yet does not stay
To ask the windows' leave to pass that way ;
Delicious deaths, soft exhalations

Of soul ; dear and divine annihilations ;
    A thousand unknown rites
      Of joys, and rarified delights ;
An hundred thousand goods, glories, and graces ;
    And many a mystic thing,
    Which the divine embraces
Of the dear Spouse of spirits, with them will bring ;
    For which it is no shame
That dull mortality must not know a name.
    Of all this store
Of blessings, and ten thousand more
    (If when He come
    He find the heart from home)
    Doubtless He will unload
    Himself some otherwhere,
    And pour abroad
    His precious sweets
On the fair soul whom first He meets.
O fair ! O fortunate ! O rich ! O dear !
    O happy and thrice-happy she,
    Dear selected dove
    Whoe'er she be,
    Whose early love
    With wingèd vows,
Makes haste to meet her morning Spouse,
And close with His immortal kisses.
    Happy indeed who never misses
    To improve that precious hour,

    And every day
    Seize her sweet prey,
All fresh and fragrant as He rises,
Dropping with a balmy shower
A delicious dew of spices ;
O let the blissful heart hold fast
Her heavenly armful ; she shall taste
At once ten thousand paradises ;
    She shall have power
    To rifle and deflower
The rich and roseal spring of those rare sweets,
Which with a swelling bosom there she meets :
Boundless and infinite, bottomless treasures
Of pure inebriating pleasures.
Happy proof ! she shall discover
    What joy, what bliss,
    How many heavens at once it is
To have her God become her Lover.

—:o:—

TO THE SAME PARTY:

Counsel Concerning her Choice.

Dear, Heaven designéd soul !
    Amongst the rest
Of suitors that besiege your maiden breast
    Why may not I
    My fortune try

And venture to speak one good word,
Not for myself, alas ! but for my dearer Lord?
You have seen already in this lower sphere
Of froth and bubbles, what to look for here :
Say, gentle soul, what can you find
      But painted shapes,
      Peacocks and apes,
      Illustrious flies,
Gilded dunghills, glorious lies ;
      Goodly surmises
      And deep disguises,
Oaths of water, words of wind ?
Truth bids me say 'tis time you cease to trust
Your soul to any son of dust.
'Tis time you listen to a braver love,
      Which from above
      Calls you up higher
      And bids you come
      And choose your room
Among His own fair sons of fire ;
      Where you among
      The golden throng,
That watches at His palace doors
      May pass along,
And follow those fair stars of yours ;
Stars much too fair and pure to wait upon
The false smiles of a sublunary sun.
Sweet, let me prophesy that at last 't will prove

PRAYER.

Your wary love
Lays up his purer and more precious vows,
And means them for a far more worthy Spouse
Than this World of lies can give ye :
Even for Him, with Whom nor cost,
Nor love, nor labour can be lost ;
Him Who never will deceive ye.
Let not my Lord, the mighty Lover
Of souls, disdain that I discover
> The hidden art
Of His high stratagem to win your heart :
>> It was His heavenly art
>> Kindly to cross you
>> In your mistaken love ;
>> That, at the next remove
>> Thence, He might toss you
>> And strike your troubled heart
Home to Himself, to hide it in His breast,
> The bright ambrosial nest
Of Love, of life, and everlasting rest.
> Happy mistake!
That thus shall wake
Your wise soul, never to be won
Now with a love below the sun.
Your first choice fails ; O when you choose again
May it not be among the sons of men !

Alexias:

THE COMPLAINT OF THE FORSAKEN WIFE OF SAINT ALEXIS.

THE FIRST ELEGY.

I, LATE the Roman youth's loved praise and pride,
Whom long none could obtain, though thousands tried;
Lo, here am left (alas!) for my lost mate
T' embrace my tears, and kiss an unkind fate.
Sure in my early woes stars were at strife,
And tried to make a widow e'er a wife.
Nor can I tell (and this new tears doth breed)
In what strange path my lord's fair footsteps bleed.
O knew I where he wander'd, I should see
Some solace in my sorrow's certainty:
I'd send my woes in words should weep for me.
(Who knows how powerful well-writ prayers would be?)
Sending's too slow a word; myself would fly.
Who knows my own heart's woes so well as I?
But how shall I steal hence? Alexis, thou,
Ah thou thyself, alas! hast taught me how.
Love too, that leads the way, would lend the wings
To bear me harmless through the hardest things
And where Love lends the wing, and leads the way,
What dangers can there be dare say me nay?
If I be shipwreck'd, Love shall teach to swim;
If drown'd, sweet is the death endured for him;
The noted sea shall change his name with me;
I 'mongst the blest stars a new name shall be;

And sure where lovers make their wat'ry graves,
The weeping mariner will augment the waves.
For who so hard, but passing by that way
Will take acquaintance of my woes, and say,
'Here 't was the Roman maid found a hard fate,
While through the World she sought her wand'ring mate ;
Here perish'd she, poor heart ; Heavens, be my vows
As true to me as she was to her spouse.
O live, so rare a love ! live ! and in thee
The too frail life of female constancy.
Farewell ; and shine, fair soul, shine there above,
Firm in thy crown, as here fast in thy love.
There thy lost fugitive thou hast found at last :
Be happy ; and for ever hold him fast.'

THE SECOND ELEGY.

Though all the joys I had fled hence with thee,
Unkind ! yet are my tears still true to me :
I'm wedded o'er again since thou art gone,
Nor couldst thou, cruel, leave me quite alone.
Alexis' widow now is Sorrow's wife ;
With him shall I weep out my weary life.
Welcome, my sad-sweet mate ! Now have I got
At last a constant Love, that leaves me not :
Firm he, as thou art false ; nor need my cries
Thus vex the Earth and tear the beauteous skies.
For him, alas ! ne'er shall I need to be
Troublesome to the world, thus, as for thee :

For thee I talk to trees; with silent groves
Expostulate my woes and much wrong'd loves.
Hills and relentless rocks, or if there be
Things that in hardness more allude to thee,
To these I talk in tears, and tell my pain,
And answer too for them in tears again.
How oft have I wept out the weary sun!
My wat'ry hour-glass hath old Time outrun.
O I am learnéd grown: poor Love and I
Have studied over all Astrology;
I'm perfect in Heaven's state, with every star
My skilful grief is grown familiar.
Rise, fairest of those fires; whate'er thou be
Whose rosy beam shall point my sun to me,
Such as the sacred light that erst did bring
The Eastern princes to their infant King.
O rise, pure lamp, and lend thy golden ray,
That weary Love at last may find his way.

THE THIRD ELEGY.

Rich, churlish Land, that hid'st so long in thee
My treasures; rich, alas, by robbing me.
Needs must my miseries owe that man a spite,
Whoe'er he be, was the first wand'ring knight.
O had he ne'er been at that cruel cost
Nature's virginity had ne'er been lost;
Seas had not been rebuked by saucy oars,
But lain lock'd up safe in their sacred shores;

Men had not spurn'd at mountains; nor made wars
With rocks, nor bold hands struck the World's strong
    bars,
Nor lost in too large bounds, our little Rome
Full sweetly with itself had dwelt at home.
My poor Alexis then, in peaceful life,
Had under some low roof loved his plain wife;
But now, ah me! from where he has no foes
He flies, and into wilful exile goes.
Cruel, return, or tell the reason why
Thy dearest parents have deserved to die.
And I, what is my crime I cannot tell,
Unless it be a crime t' have loved too well.
If heats of holier love and high desire
Make big thy fair breast with immortal fire,
What needs my virgin lord fly thus from me,
Who only wish his virgin wife to be?
Witness, chaste Heavens! no happier vows I know
Than to a virgin grave untouch'd to go.
Love's truest knot by Venus is not tied;
Nor do embraces only make a bride.
The queen of angels (and men chaste as you)
Was maiden-wife, and maiden-mother too.
Cecilia, glory of her name and blood,
With happy gain her maiden vows made good.
The lusty bridegroom made approach—'Young man,
Take heed' (said she) ' take heed, Valerian!
My bosom's guard, a spirit great and strong,

Stands arm'd to shield me from all wanton wrong.
My chastity is sacred ; and my Sleep
Wakeful, her dear vows undefiled to keep.
Pallas bears arms, forsooth ; and should there be
No fortress built for true Virginity ?
No gaping Gorgon this : none like the rest
Of your learn'd lies.   Here you'll find no such jest.
I 'm yours : O were my God, my Christ so too,
I 'd know no name of Love on Earth but you.'
He yields, and straight baptized, obtains the grace
To gaze on the fair soldier's glorious face.
Both mix'd at last their blood in one rich bed
Of rosy martyrdom, twice married.
O burn our Hymen bright in such high flame,
Thy torch, terrestrial Love, has here no name.
How sweet the mutual yoke of man and wife,
When holy fires maintain Love's heavenly life !
But I (so help me Heaven my hopes to see),
When thousands sought my love, loved none but thee.
Still, as their vain tears my firm vows did try,
' Alexis, he alone is mine' (said I).
Half true, alas ! half false, proves that poor line,
Alexis is alone ; but is not mine.

Description of a Religious House and Condition of Life.

(OUT OF BARCLAY.)

No roofs of gold o'er riotous tables shining,
Whole days and suns devour'd with endless dining.
No sails of Tyrian silk, proud pavements sweeping,
Nor ivory couches costlier slumber keeping;
False lights of flaring gems; tumultuous joys;
Halls full of flattering men and frisking boys;
Whate'er false shows of short and slippery good
Mix the mad sons of men in mutual blood.
But walks and unshorn woods; and souls, just so
Unforced and genuine; but not shady though.
Our lodgings hard and homely as our fare,
That chaste and cheap, as the few clothes we wear;
Those, coarse and negligent, as the natural locks
Of these loose groves; rough as th' unpolish'd rocks.
A hasty portion of prescribèd sleep;
Obedient slumbers, that can wake and weep,
And sing, and sigh, and work, and sleep again;
Still rolling a round sphere of still-returning pain.
Hands full of hearty labours; pains that pay
And prize themselves; do much, that more they may,
And work for work, not wages; let to-morrow's
New drops, wash off the sweat of this day's sorrows.
A long and daily-dying life, which breathes
A respiration of reviving deaths.

But neither are there those ignoble stings
That nip the blossom of the World's best things,
And lash Earth-labouring souls. . . .
No cruel guard of diligent cares, that keep
Crown'd woes awake, as things too wise for sleep :
But reverent discipline, and religious fear,
And soft obedience, find sweet biding here ;
Silence, and sacred rest ; peace, and pure joys :
Kind loves keep house, lie close, make no noise ;
And room enough for monarchs, while none swells
Beyond the kingdoms of contentful cells.
The self-rememb'ring soul sweetly recovers
Her kindred with the stars ; not basely hovers
Below : but meditates her immortal way
Home to the original source of Light and intellectual day.

—:o:—

An Epitaph Upon a Young Married Couple,

DEAD AND BURIED TOGETHER.

To these, whom Death again did wed,
This grave's their second marriage-bed ;
For though the hand of Fate could force
'Twixt soul and body, a divorce,
It could not sunder man and wife,
'Cause they both lived but one life.
Peace, good Reader, do not weep.

Peace, the lovers are asleep !
They, sweet turtles, folded lie
In the last knot that Love could tie.
And though they lie as they were dead,
Their pillow stone, their sheets of lead :
(Pillow hard, and sheets not warm)
Love made the bed ; they'll take no harm ;
Let them sleep : let them sleep on,
Till this stormy night be gone,
And the eternal morrow dawn ;
Then the curtains will be drawn
And they wake into a light,
Whose Day shall never sleep in Night.

—:o:- -

Death's Lecture and the Funeral of a Young Gentleman.

DEAR relics of a dislodged soul, whose lack
Makes many a mourning paper put on black !
O stay a while, ere thou draw in thy head,
And wind thyself up close in thy cold bed.
Stay but a little while, until I call
A summons worthy of thy funeral.
Come then, Youth, Beauty, and Blood, all ye soft powers,
Whose silken flatteries swell a few fond hours
Into a false eternity. Come man ;
Hyperbolisèd nothing ! know thy span !

Take thine own measure here, down, down, and bow
Before thyself in thine idea ; thou
Huge emptiness ! contract thy bulk ; and shrink
All thy wild circle to a point.   O sink
Lower and lower yet ; till thy small size,
Call Heaven to look on thee with narrow eyes.
Lesser and lesser yet ; till thou begin
To show a face, fit to confess thy kin,
Thy neighbourhood to Nothing !
Proud looks, and lofty eyelids, here put on
Yourselves in your unfeign'd reflection ;
Here, gallant ladies ! this unpartial glass
(Through all your painting) shows you your true face.
These death-seal'd lips are they dare give the lie
To the loud boasts of poor Mortality ;
These curtain'd windows, this retired eye
Out-stares the lids of large-look'd Tyranny :
This posture is the brave one ; this that lies
Thus low, stands up (methinks) thus, and defies
The World.   All-daring dust and ashes ! only you
Of all interpreters read Nature true.

Temperance.

OF THE CHEAP PHYSICIAN, UPON THE TRANSLATION OF LESSIUS.

Go now, with some daring drug,
Bait thy disease, and while they tug,
Thou, to maintain their cruel strife
Spend the dear treasure of thy life:
Go take physic, doat upon
Some big-named composition,—
The oraculous doctors' mystic bills,
Certain hard words made into pills;
And what at length shalt get by these?
Only a costlier disease.
Go poor man, think what shall be
Remedy 'gainst thy remedy.
That which makes us have no need
Of physic, that's physic indeed.

    Hark hither, Reader: wouldst thou see
Nature her own physician be?
Wouldst see a man all his own wealth,
His own music, his own health?
A man, whose sober soul can tell
How to wear her garments well?
Her garments that upon her sit,
(As garments should do) close and fit?
A well-clothed soul, that's not oppress'd
Nor choked with what she should be dress'd?
Whose soul's sheath'd in a crystal shrine,

Through which all her bright features shine?
As when a piece of wanton lawn,
A thin aerial veil is drawn,
O'er Beauty's face; seeming to hide,
More sweetly shews the blushing bride:
A soul, whose intellectual beams
No mists do mask, no lazy steams?
A happy soul, that all the way
To Heaven, hath a Summer's day?
Wouldst see a man whose well-warm'd blood
Bathes him in a genuine flood?
A man, whose tunèd humours be
A set of rarest harmony?
Wouldst see blithe looks, fresh cheeks, beguile
Age? Wouldst see December smile?
Wouldst see a nest of roses grow
In a bed of rev'rend snow?
Warm thoughts, free spirits, flattering
Winter's self into a Spring?
In sum, wouldst see a man that can
Live to be old, and still a man?
Whose latest, and most leaden hours
Fall with soft wings, stuck with soft flowers;
And when Life's sweet fable ends,
His soul and body part like friends:
No quarrels, murmurs, no delay:
A kiss, a sigh, and so away?
This rare one, Reader, wouldst thou see,
Hark hither: and thyself be he!

hope.

    Hope, whose weak being ruin'd is
Alike, if it succeed, or if it miss!
Whom ill and good doth equally confound,
And both the horns of Fate's dilemma wound.
      Vain shadow; that dost vanish quite
      Both at full noon, and perfect night!
      The stars have not a possibility
      Of blessing thee.
If things then from their end we happy call,
'Tis Hope is the most hopeless thing of all.

    Hope, thou bold taster of delight!
Who instead of doing so, devour'st it quite.
Thou bring'st us an estate, yet leav'st us poor
By clogging it with legacies before.
      The joys which we entire should wed,
      Come deflowr'd virgins to our bed.
      Good fortunes without gain imported be,
      Such mighty custom's paid to thee;
For joy, like wine kept close, doth better taste;
If it take air before his spirits waste.

    Hope, Fortune's cheating lottery,
Where, for one prize, an hundred blanks there be.
Fond archer, Hope! who tak'st thine aim so far,
That still, or short, or wide, thine arrows are;
      Thin empty cloud which th' eye deceives

With shapes that our own fancy gives.
A cloud, which gilt and painted now appears,
But must drop presently in tears :
When thy false beams o'er reason's light prevail,
By ignes fatui for North stars we sail.

Brother of Fear! more gaily clad,
The merrier fool o' th' two, yet quite as mad ;
Sire of Repentance! child of fond desire,
That blow'st the chymic's, and the lover's fire.
Still leading them insensibly on,
With the strange witchcraft of 'anon'
By thee the one does changing Nature, through
Her endless labyrinths pursue ;
And th' other chases woman ; while she goes
More ways and turns than hunted Nature knows.

M. COWLEY.

—:o:—

M. Crashaw's Answer for Hope.

Dear Hope! Earth's dow'ry, and Heaven's debt!
The entity of things that are not yet.
Subtlest, but surest being! thou by whom
Our nothing has a definition!
  Substantial shade! whose sweet allay
  Blends both the noons of Night and Day :
  Fates cannot find out a capacity
  Of hurting thee.

From thee their lean dilemma, with blunt horn,
Shrinks as the sick moon from the wholesome morn.

   Rich hope! Love's legacy, under lock
Of Faith!—still spending, and still growing stock!
Our crown-land lies above, yet each meal brings
A seemly portion for the sons of kings.
     Nor will the virgin-joys we wed
     Come less unbroken to our bed,
     Because that from the bridal cheek of Bliss,
     Thou steal'st us down a distant kiss.
Hope's chaste stealth harms no more Joy's maidenhead
Than spousal rites prejudge the marriage-bed.

   Fair hope! our earlier Heav'n! by thee
Young time is taster to Eternity:
Thy generous wine with age grows strong, not sour,
Nor does it kill thy fruit, to smell thy flower.
     Thy golden growing head never hangs down,
     Till in the lap of Love's full noon
     It falls; and dies! O no, it melts away
     As doth the dawn into the Day:
As lumps of sugar loose themselves, and twine
Their subtle essence with the soul of wine.

   Fortune? alas, above the World's low wars
Hope walks and kicks the curl'd heads of conspiring stars.
Her keel cuts not the waves where our winds stir,
Fortune's whole lottery is one blank to her.

Her shafts and she fly far above,
   And forage in the fields of light and love.
Sweet Hope! kind cheat! fair fallacy! by thee
   We are not where nor what we be,
But what and where we would be.   Thus art thou
Our absent presence, and our future now.

   Faith's sister! nurse of fair desire!
Fear's antidote! a wise and well-staid fire!
Temper 'twixt chill Despair, and torrid Joy!
Queen regent in young Love's minority!
   Though the vext chymic vainly chases
   His fugitive gold through all her faces;
Though Love's more fierce, more fruitless fires assay:
   One face more fugitive than all they;
True Hope's a glorious huntress, and her chase,
   The God of Nature in the fields of grace.

Glossary.

Alas (*Answer for Hope*), an exclamation merely.
Conduct (*To the Name of Jesus*), train.
God of flies (*Prayer*), Satan.
Deliquium (*Glor. Epiph.*), faint, swoon.
Embrave (*New Year's Day*), decorate.
Field's eyes (*S. Mary Magd.*), flowers.
Gold (*S. Mary Magd.*), Magdalene's golden hair.
Indifferent (*Glor. Epiph.*), impartial.
"Ite" (*Dies Irae*), "go ye."
Legible (*Glor. Epiph.*), for legibly.
Nuzzled (*S. Mary Magd.*), nestled.
Officious (*Hol. Nativity*), willing to do good offices.
Paramours (*New Year's Day*), lovers.
Ports (*S. Thomas*), gates or doors.
Solicitors (*To the Name of Jesus*), exciters or animators.
Transumed (*Lauda Sion Salvatorem*), to take from one to another; to convert.
Tree (*Sancta Maria Dol.*), the Cross.

Index to the First Lines.

	PAGE
Bright Babe, Whose awful beauties make	22
Come, we shepherds, whose blest sight	15
Dear, Heaven-designèd soul!	103
Dear Hope! Earth's dowry and Heaven's debt!	118
Dear relics of a dislodged soul, whose lack	113
Go now, with some daring drug	115
Hail, most High, most humble one!	70
Hail, sister springs!	75
Hark! she is called, the parting hour is come	72
Hear'st thou, my soul, what serious things	67
Here, where our Lord once laid His head	46
Hope, whose weak being ruined is	117
How life and death in Thee	48
I, late the Roman youth's loved praise and pride	106
In shade of Death's sad tree	52
I sing the name which none can say	6
Jesu, no more! It is full tide	57
Know'st thou this, Soldier? 'tis a much changed plant, which yet	59
Lo, here a little volume, but great book!	99
Look up, languishing soul! Lo, where the fair	46
Lord, by Thy sweet and saving sign	33
Lord, what is man? why should he cost Thee	49
Lord, when the sense of Thy sweet grace	98
Love, thou art absolute sole Lord	85
'Mongst those long rows of crowns that gild your race	32
No roofs of gold o'er riotous tables shining	111
Rich, churlish Land, that hid'st so long in thee	108
Rise, royal Sion! rise and sing	63

Rise, thou best and brightest morning!	20
These Hours, and that which hovers o'er my end	45
They have left Thee naked, Lord; O that they had!	60
Though all the joys I had fled hence with thee	107
Thus have I back again to thy bright name	92
To these, whom Death again did wed	112
'Twixt pen and pencil rose a holy strife	3
Was Car then Crashawe: or was Crashawe Car	1
Well-meaning readers! You that come as friends	94
What heaven-entreated heart is this	4
With all the powers my poor heart hath	60

www.ingramcontent.com/pod-product-compliance
Lightning Source LLC
Chambersburg PA
CBHW020054170426
43199CB00009B/276